"Every now and then I come across a book that I wish had [...] de-
cades ago. As the father of two grown children, this is certainly one of them.
From two very different pathways that led to Christ as their shared destination and home, the McAllisters write with truth, frankness, and hope for
all who are eager to parent their children well (or, perhaps better said, to not
mess our children up too much). As I look back on my own parenting, this
father-son duo has helped me see that even our greatest mistakes are not only
covered but can be turned to good. Why? Because, as they demonstrate in
these pages, successful parenting is more about humility and surrender than
it is about 'getting it right.' I highly recommend this book."

Scott Sauls, senior pastor of Christ Presbyterian Church in Nashville, Tennessee,
and author of *Jesus Outside the Lines*

"Far too many young people abandon Christianity as they enter their teenage
years, and all too often, families struggle with how to help their children
sustain their faith into adulthood. In this thoughtful and insightful book,
Cameron McAllister and Stuart McAllister present a solid framework for
personal spiritual formation and developing the culture of the home that
provides conditions for robust and lasting faith. There are no quick fixes
offered here, and that's all to the good; instead, the son-and-father writers
provide a model of how to do the hard, necessary, and rewarding work of
discipleship in the family."

Holly Ordway, Fellow of Faith and Culture at the Word on Fire Institute and author
of *Apologetics and the Christian Imagination*

"The McAllisters have crafted a candid and unassuming look into a father-son
relationship that helps us see what redemption truly looks like in a fallen
world. Their story centers on a single life-changing question, 'Son, why do you
call yourself a Christian?' As both sides of this one question unfold, we are
invited to a thriving, maturing faith that is as realistic and messy as it is
necessary and life giving. Beautifully written, relatable, and accessible, this
work will be one that is timeless in its influence."

Mary Jo Sharp, assistant professor of apologetics at Houston Baptist University

"Rich, wise, and eminently helpful, *Faith That Lasts* is magnificent. It speaks
to the heart of the challenging problem of handing on the torch of faith, and
its father-son authorship is the best demonstration of the success of the
counsel they offer."

Os Guinness, author of *The Call: Finding and Fulfilling God's Purpose in Your Life*

"Within today's shifting, superficial culture, our children are desperately searching for something solid, true, meaningful, and enduring. Countering quick fixes and fearful responses, Stuart and Cameron McAllister provide a much-needed correction to our superficial view of Christian parenting. Through scriptural wisdom and their own lived experience, they call us toward intentional, embodied understanding of life within the deep riches of Christ. This book is essential reading for any parent who wants to live and pass along a lasting faith to their children."

Jana Harmon, adjunct professor of cultural apologetics at Biola University and teaching fellow at the C. S. Lewis Institute of Atlanta

"This is a valuable and much-needed book for Christian parents who want to raise their children to know and follow Christ. It gives a very helpful account of how two Christian parents applied godly wisdom in shepherding their son's heart through the ups and downs of his journey to Christ while living in secular Europe and amid the cultural Christianity of the American South. It also provides important insights into today's toxic culture and how to avoid three well-meaning but ineffective strategies for helping our children stay faithful. I wish I had read something like this when I was raising my children. Highly recommended!"

Thomas Tarrants, president emeritus of the C. S. Lewis Institute

FAITH THAT LASTS

A FATHER AND SON ON
CULTIVATING LIFELONG BELIEF

CAMERON McALLISTER
AND STUART McALLISTER

An imprint of InterVarsity Press
Downers Grove, Illinois

InterVarsity Press
P.O. Box 1400, Downers Grove, IL 60515-1426
ivpress.com
email@ivpress.com

*InterVarsity Press® is the book-publishing division of InterVarsity Christian Fellowship/USA®,
a movement of students and faculty active on campus at hundreds of universities, colleges, and schools
of nursing in the United States of America, and a member movement of the International Fellowship of
Evangelical Students. For information about local and regional activities, visit intervarsity.org.*

*Scripture quotations, unless otherwise noted, are from The Holy Bible, English Standard Version, copyright
© 2001 by Crossway Bibles, a division of Good News Publishers. Used by permission. All rights reserved.*

*While any stories in this book are true, some names and identifying information may have been changed
to protect the privacy of individuals.*

Cover design and image composite: David Fassett
Interior design: Daniel van Loon
*Images: clouds: © Merethe Svarstad Eeg / EyEm / Getty Images
        balancing stones: © Radoslav Zilinsky / Moment Collection / Getty Images*

ISBN 978-0-8308-4814-0 (print)
ISBN 978-0-8308-4815-7 (digital)

Printed in the United States of America ♾

*InterVarsity Press is committed to ecological stewardship and to the conservation of natural resources
in all our operations. This book was printed using sustainably sourced paper.*

Library of Congress Cataloging-in-Publication Data
A catalog record for this book is available from the Library of Congress.

P	25	24	23	22	21	20	19	18	17	16	15	14	13	12	11	10	9	8	7	6	5	4	3	2	1
Y	39	38	37	36	35	34	33	32	31	30	29	28	27	26	25	24		23		22		21			

For Dylan,

may you fail successfully, love virtuously, and imitate righteously.

—Cameron

I would like to dedicate this book to my incredibly generous wife, Mary. Her vision, her love for the family, her use of meals and hospitality, and her creation of a place that was always a real home was the cradle from which much here could be written. None of it would have happened without you. I am deeply grateful and thank God for you. May this book be an encouragement to you as you have been to all of us.

Proverbs 31:29-31 says it better than I can.

—Stuart

CONTENTS

FOREWORD

Chris Brooks

I was an expert at parenting . . . before I had children!

When my wife, Yodit, and I married, few things were as certain in our hearts as having a big family. We prayed that the Lord would bless us with precisely six children. I am still not sure how we arrived at that exact number. But, in the early days of our marriage, we settled on having three boys and three girls. We were confident that the beautifully symmetrical vision we had for our future family was God's plan for us. We even went as far as deciding on each of their names. My overconfidence in my parental abilities extended well beyond simply identifying cute names for our yet-to-be-born children. In those preparenting days, I could also tell you, with great pride, the sure-fire plan I had for shaping my children spiritually, as well.

While we were still anticipating children, I would sometimes daydream about what our family worship times were assured to look like. In the "Thomas Kinkade–esque" portrait of my mind I am sitting in a handcrafted rocking chair, finely dressed, wearing my favorite ascot and smoking jacket, while holding a freshly bound leather Bible in my hands. In this imaginary scene, Yodit would use her melodious voice to lead our well-groomed children and me in a beautiful hymn. All six of our kids would be perfectly manicured, sitting quietly with full attentiveness, pleasant smiles, and in total compliance with our every command. As I opened my Bible to the perfect passage of Scripture, a beam of golden sunlight would come rushing through the window of our cottage-style home and land softly on the page that I was reading. I would teach an impeccable devotional lesson. My wife and kids would be in awe of my spiritual brilliance and quickly affirm that my insights were directly from the Lord. I would, of course, agree with their assessment. We would then have one of our "just-shy-of-perfect" children say a closing prayer in which they would express tremendous gratitude over the sheer privilege of being a member of such a splendid family.

Looking back, I laugh (as I am sure that you are as well) at how wonderfully naive I was and how hopelessly foolish my foolproof plan would prove to be. It would not be long before God burst my little fantasy family bubble with something that was far less my ideal and far more his perfect plan for us. What I didn't know then, but I do now, is that God was taking two partially formed lumps of clay and forming us on his potter's wheel into something beautiful. His process would take more time than we had hoped and be far more painful than we ever could have imagined. He would shape us by using the type of blows that come only from the gentle but firm hands of a master sculptor and a loving Father.

It would be seven years before God would bless us with our first child. Christopher would come to our family through the beauty of adoption. He was seventeen and we were a very young twenty-seven. How his adoption came about is an account far too long and intimate for these pages, but suffice it to say that God was writing our family's love story in amazing yet unexpected ways. When we opened our home and hearts to Christopher, it was clear that this was God's plan for our family. It was also quickly clear that, while we were overjoyed that God had called us to be Chris's parents, we were in over our heads.

I was an inexperienced dad, whose attempts at discipleship, though sincere, often failed because they were riddled with false assumptions. My first assumption was that I could simply teach my son into Christlike character and maturity. I had not yet learned the artful skill of catechism, and Chris wasn't interested in my well-formed lesson plans; he wanted to have real talks about his doubts and struggles with sin. But unfortunately, my fears of inadequacy seemed to prevent me from having the type of deeply honest and transparent conversations that his soul so desperately longed for. Our devotional times didn't look anything like a Thomas Kinkade–inspired painting. They were messy and looked more like they were ripped out of a kids' coloring book most days, and I was certainly coloring outside the lines.

Looking back, I lament that there were many days when I seemed to push Chris further away from me and from Christ by using a fear-based parenting approach. Not that I was threatening or overbearing in my fathering of Chris, I just falsely assumed that a fire and brimstone, "scared-straight" method of discipleship that was centered more on the consequences of his mistakes than on the all-sufficient grace of God was the right way of dealing with deeply rooted sin patterns. I am not sure why I assumed this would work for him, because it certainly had not worked in my life. Chris had rightly looked to me to help him with the internal battles he had warred against his entire life, and regrettably I had applied a shallow remedy instead of delving deep into his heart. I would later discover that helping him to find the freedom he had longed for would require something of far greater substance, and it would also transform me in the process.

I wish I had at my fingertips then the type of book that you are currently reading. Don't get me wrong, Christ was certainly gracious to my son and me. In our sincere pursuit of him, his loving hand guided us to real spiritual breakthroughs. In spite of my ill-conceived plans, we were blessed to stumble upon our fair share of victories along the way. But these wins only came when I was humble enough to do away with my erroneous preconceived notions about parenting and what it meant to cultivate a heart for Christ in my child. My hope in sharing my own mistakes and failures is to help other fathers and sons avoid them.

We all need a blueprint for navigating the unknowns of the parent-child faith journey. I can't think of two better tour guides than Stuart and Cameron McAllister. Rarely do you find two people whose intellects are matched by their genuine character and humility. Typically, men avoid being vulnerable, in fear that our shortcomings, when exposed, will cause us to lose credibility. But I am convinced that Stuart and Cameron have discovered that Christ's strength is truly made perfect in our weaknesses and that his grace is sufficient for the challenges that come along with building a faith that lasts from one generation to the next. To be sure, their insights will disrupt your assumptions, but in the process, you will become the type of person that God uses to pass authentic faith to your son(s) and daughter(s).

In 2019 my son Chris passed away unexpectedly from pneumonia. Losing him is the deepest sadness of my heart. But the greatest joy of my heart is knowing the real and vibrant faith he grew to possess and the mutual love we shared for knowing Christ. Chris excelled at showing others the truth, beauty, and justice of Jesus through his words and deeds. As his dad I grew to admire the type of nonpretentious, compassion-driven, unapologetically honest faith he demonstrated. Reflecting back, I am clear that once we embraced many of the truths the McAllisters have written about in this book, our discipleship relationship flourished. Today my message to parents is that there are no honorable mentions when it comes to passing your faith to your children. You cannot outsource building a spiritual legacy, but you can apply the timely wisdom of *Faith That Lasts* to shape your children for Jesus. So let the journey begin!

INTRODUCTION

Your Home Has a Culture
(Whether You Like It or Not)

*You shall be holy to me, for I the LORD am holy and have
separated you from the peoples, that you should be mine.*

LEVITICUS 20:26

W. H. Auden observed that "It takes little talent to see clearly
what lies under one's nose, a good deal of it to know in
which direction to point that organ."[1] In this book we're going to
suggest that Christians should begin by looking at their homes.
The home is, of course, much more than a habitat or a mere physical
shelter. We need a more capacious word to capture its essence: a
home is a *place*. It's a place with a wealth of sights, smells, textures,
and memories. Moreover, it's always a haunted place—a place
where the departed continue to smile at us from framed pictures,
where we hear the echoes of laughter and feel the tension of lin-
gering arguments, a place filled with the fragrance of past meals
and mountains of dishes in the sink. In short, it's a place filled with
the evidence of human life in all its messy and mysterious glory.

From the emergency stashes of cigarettes and junk food to the
items in the search histories of our devices, our homes are also
places filled with secrets. In a deep sense, if we want to know about

our true religion—"the shape of our ultimate concern"—we need to look no further than our homes, especially their hidden nooks and crannies.[2] It's a sobering thought, but nothing tells the story of our actual convictions like the places we live, and these convictions are often spelled out most clearly in the spaces we think no one sees. Consequently, most homes have a two-tier culture, one where the surfaces are always dusted and the sheets are always turned down, and the other where we do our actual living.

Christ offers a vivid picture to illustrate this common divide between appearances and reality: Those who invest all of their energies in outward appearances are tantamount to people who clean only the "outside of the cup and the plate" (Matthew 23:25-26). It's a shrewd observation that flows directly from the biblical emphasis on a person's inward condition: "Keep your heart with all vigilance, for from it flow the springs of life" (Proverbs 4:23). Concerning many so-called Christian homes, devotion to Christ is often a matter of mere ornamentation—a framed verse or a decorative cross above the living room sofa. But if we look at the state of our relationship with God, our marriages, our relationships with our children, and the manifold addictions we can't seem to shake, it's clear that we often clean only the outside of our homes while neglecting the inside. That is, according to our Lord, our homes often fall prey to an outside-of-the-cup culture, all shiny exteriors and festering interiors.

Since *culture* is such an overused word, let's venture a modest definition. Broadly speaking, culture is "a way of life lived in common," to borrow Os Guinness's phrase.[3] This response includes everything from music and poetry to architecture and food. Naturally, time levels a good deal of the culture of the past. What does survive, however, often serves as both a treasure and a relic. Consider the vast distance between an ancient cathedral and a skyscraper and you'll have an idea of the rapidly shifting mindsets surrounding our achievements. Given time's speed and ruthlessness, we rightfully cherish those voices and institutions that survive its ravages. Thus we often call these survivors "timeless," whether they be symphonies or Sistine ceilings. Unlike most of the hallmarks of a given era, these achievements seem to lack expiration dates. They are courses in a seemingly inexhaustible banquet for humanity. But as much as we treasure the legacy of our abiding achievements, we know that everything—even the Sistine Chapel—has an expiration date. Ultimately, no human culture is immune to the ravages of time.

"In the beginning was the Word, and the Word was with God, and the Word was God. He was in the beginning with God. All things were made through him, and without him was not any thing made that was made" (John 1:1-3). This majestic opening to John's Gospel firmly establishes Christ's supremacy over all creation. When this divine Word becomes flesh and sets foot on the stage of his creation, we see that he alone can transcend its limitations. Shakespeare may boast of "eternal lines"[4] that forever preserve his beloved for the world, but Christ alone can say, "Before Abraham was, I am" (John 8:58). It is this eternal Word who established his church on earth. Consequently, those who belong to him are not simply card-carrying members of yet another passing cultural institution. Rather, they are parts of his eternal body: "You are the body of Christ and individually members of it" (1 Corinthians 12:27). Herein lies the central tension of being in but not of the world: Christian men and women are members of an eternal body who for the time being must make their homes in a temporal place.

Given these portentous claims, what exactly distinguishes a Christian home? Does it shine like a miniature city on a hill? Does it glow with the angelic light of a Thomas Kinkade painting? Do its members lead quiet lives of perpetual comfort and stability?

Here's the way it's supposed to be: Christians ought to cultivate homes that reflect their membership in the household of God (1 Timothy 3:15). If culture is indeed a way of life lived in common, consider Paul's lovely description of the common life of the church:

> Let the word of Christ dwell in you richly, teaching and admonishing one another in all wisdom, singing psalms and hymns and spiritual songs, with thankfulness in your hearts to God. And whatever you do, in word or deed, do everything in the name of the Lord Jesus, giving thanks to God the Father through him. (Colossians 3:16-17)

Sadly, we often underestimate the insidious nature of the world outside the church, and our households end up paying lip service to the gospel while walking in lockstep with the surrounding culture.

We're not naive; we understand that you make your home in the twenty-first-century world and that this particular era, like all eras in human history, carries a unique set of challenges. Though we don't claim to be exhaustive, we'd like to offer three arguments regarding the home that we hope will help to make sense of the strange place we live: (1) Far from being airtight shelters from the world, our homes are porous and highly susceptible to outside influences. (2) Though it often goes unrecognized, the key influence shaping our homes is always a story. (3) The true distinguishing factor of Christian homes is not that they are free from significant hardship and adversity, but that they're shaped by the story of Christ and his coming kingdom.

Here's the bad news: If we've bought into the notion that mere intellectual assent to the gospel makes our home immune to the surrounding cultural forces, chances are those forces have already thoroughly shaped our homes. As we'll see in chapter two, it's more than possible to master the language of Christianity while giving our hearts to something else entirely. For the time being, it's worth noting that this assumption is itself a peculiarly American pathology; we might call it the tradition of no traditions. The ironic truth is that Christians who believe their homes to be shelters from the world often mirror its deepest assumptions in myriad ways they don't even recognize, let alone understand. That is, they're shaped by a story that's profoundly at odds with the gospel. In the end the assumption that a home has no culture simply leads to cultural assimilation. Consequently, many so-called Christian homes already belong to the very culture they wish to challenge. For this reason many young people believe they're outgrowing Christianity when in fact they're simply outgrowing a cultural husk that's easily discarded when they face the onslaught of life's many challenges. Our book aims to show that, while it's impossible to outgrow authentic Christianity, the Americanized spin on the gospel is a hollow shell that doesn't survive spiritual maturity.

The good news is that Christian homes have and always will withstand the gales of cultural opposition because they are defined first and foremost by Christ and his church. Theirs is the story of the crucified and risen Lord who is returning to judge the living and the dead. Thus Christian homes are inhabited by men and women who see their surrounding world from the standpoint of eternity—the men and women who are the true realists about the human story. The three arguments that follow will provide a kind of map of the deeply strange and challenging world where we make our homes.

POROUS SELVES IN POROUS HOMES

As we gaze out on a landscape that looks increasingly dystopian, many of us worry that we're already living in Aldous Huxley's *Brave New World*. If the 2020 pandemic made our world look like the scenery in a sci-fi story, we could always turn back to our entertainment for confirmation. From the bleak worlds of *Black Mirror* and *The Handmaid's Tale* to the posthuman musings of the *Terminator* franchise and *Blade Runner*, we don't stop worrying about our Huxleyan condition when we kick back on the couch.

Because the cultural landscape is so surreal, our most incisive thinkers are resorting to increasingly creative strategies for describing it. For instance, the Canadian philosopher Charles Taylor's monumental work *A Secular Age* offers a dense array of exotic terms and concepts for capturing our present moment: "immanent frame," "buffered self," "closed world structures," and "nova effect." At times, his narrative reads like a sophisticated sci-fi novel.[5] Though it's initially a bit overwhelming, once these concepts sink in, they can help us make sense of the bizarre place in which we make our homes. A story from Cameron's early adulthood will help to make this clear.

Cameron worked as a cashier at a grocery store when he was in college. It was the kind of job that makes shy and deeply introverted persons flee to personality tests to prove that something isn't wrong with us. "Good afternoon, ma'am. Find everything all right?" "I'm sorry, sir. This is an express lane." What's so hard about that? Just stick to the script.

But customers never stick to the script, especially when the store is thronged and the lines are bulging with disgruntled folks coming home from disgruntled offices. During these barrages, Cameron would console himself with a distinctly modern myth: he'd tell himself that his body was a kind of organic fortress behind which his true essence (his mind) was protected. If it was a particularly trying day, this fantasy grew more and more elaborate, transforming his body into a highly specialized machine with a soul at its helm. This mechanistic conception comes to us courtesy of French philosopher René Descartes.[6] If you've got some Hollywood imagery in your head, this only further illustrates how deeply we've internalized this Cartesian vision. Think of Sigourney Weaver donning the P-5000 Work Loader, an industrial exoskeleton, in order to do combat with the enormous queen alien in James Cameron's *Aliens*.

Charles Taylor has a name for this modern fantasy: "The buffered self" pictures us as "insulated in an interior 'mind'" and thus shielded from any outside forces.[7] In Taylor's words, "For the modern, buffered self, the possibility exists of taking a distance from, disengaging from everything outside the mind. My ultimate purposes are those which arise within me, the crucial meanings of things are those defined by my responses to them."[8]

While the phrase may sound outlandish, a number of our everyday practices quickly show its practicality. Think about our habit of avoiding the threat of chatty neighbors on public transportation with noise-canceling headphones. Or the even more common habit of falling through the digital trapdoor of our phones whenever we want to escape from our surroundings. It's especially unnerving that our phones often help us escape the people we love the most. Whether it's phones, tablets, or Bluetooth headsets, our public spaces are increasingly filled with people hiding behind their respective digital fortresses.[9]

A sobering confirmation of this fact arrived one afternoon when Cameron—long out of the grocery business—found himself in his toddler's room assuming that most modern of poses: supine, one arm raised in a kind of supplicating gesture while holding his talismanic phone above his yearning face. Meanwhile, his little boy just wanted the attention of his father. If this scene were captured by a painter or a photographer, it would serve as a grim picture of our self-imposed loneliness and isolation. A disturbing question occurred to Cameron: *Why am I using my phone to hide from my son?*

One of the paradoxes of our digital world is that it makes us feel simultaneously invincible and more vulnerable than ever. On the one hand, from smartphones to tablets the unvoiced assumption seems to be that technology functions as a kind of specialized armor, keeping us invincible to the world around us. Philosophers often use the prospect of invisibility to explore the thornier challenges of personal integrity. How would *you* behave if *you* were invisible? Would you show restraint, or would this new power lead to ethical compromises?

So far, no direct physical invisibility technology is available to us. However, our online interactions betray what can only be called an invisibility mindset. We traverse the online spaces like ghosts, freely spying on the numerous lives and conversations in our orbit. We also exhibit an increasing lack of restraint—one that leads to escalating levels of tension and outright hostility. It's a kind of animosity that resembles road rage in its ability to transform seemingly polite, mild-mannered folks into salivating paroxysms of rage. You can almost see people foaming at the mouth behind their screens. The anonymity of the online world only compounds the issue. There's a reason more and more websites are disabling their comment sections. How many of us have lost friends because all manners, all social decorum, and all decency went out the window in the online jungle? The sobering fact is that many of us act like unhinged invisible people when we're online, believing that our technological armor protects us from the risks of face-to-face interactions.

But our technology also makes us more vulnerable than ever. We've already mentioned the damage to our friendships, but let's not overlook our careers and reputations. How many careers have been derailed because of one thoughtless post? For that matter, how many of us have suffered at the invisible hands of a digital mob? What about campaigns of online persecution? As we'll see later, the digital world also tends to foster a deep-seated craving for constant affirmation and personal validation. When it's absent, many of us move from dejection to despair. Never has such apparent invulnerability given rise to such intense frailty.

A more insidious form of vulnerability is our near-total dependence on our machines. It's revealing that many of our post-apocalyptic nightmares turn on the failures of technology. For many of us it's the end of the world when things break. There's a level of truth to these fears: the most influential and lasting innovations are usually irreversible in the sense that they're now integral parts of our society's function. While it's technically true that we don't need cars, the consequences would be catastrophic if they were somehow subtracted from our world. The same goes for the World Wide Web.[10] A severed internet connection is a kind of existential crisis. When a landscaper delivered the fateful news to Stuart's wife, Mary, that he and his crew had accidentally severed their internet cable, it brought the McAllister household to a temporary standstill—the end of the world in microcosm.

In sharp contrast to Cameron's mechanized daydreams, Stuart had an unnerving encounter in his pre-Christian years that forever shattered his illusions regarding the "buffered self." Stuart and a group of spiritually intrepid friends gathered around a Ouija board in an effort to channel the spirit of a recently departed friend of a famous actor. All the initially ominous feeling soon gave way to disappointment and vague embarrassment. Nothing was happening. A Ouija board is, after all, only a board game. How was it different from any of the other games that littered our closets? And what were they, a group of scientifically minded kids, doing with this outdated ritual anyway?

Then things suddenly got out of control. The temperature plummeted, and a malign presence announced itself when one of the men in the group was lifted into the air and thrown across the room. The group was petrified. They quickly blew out all of the candles, opened the windows, and fled into the street. This was hardly a spiritual experience on par with what people experienced in the ancient world. The group viewed the ritual as little more than a game with some potential thrills involved—more experimentation than belief—and they certainly had no intention of following the logic of what happened back to a real, dark power and the possibility of God.

Still, though not yet a Christian, Stuart wasn't able to shake the conviction that he and his friends had just learned firsthand the immortal lesson from Shakespeare's *Hamlet*: "There are more things in heaven and on earth, Horatio, / Than are dreamt of in your philosophy."[11] There was more to the world than met the eye, and the self was not invulnerable to this truth.

Taylor's phrase for this mindset is the "porous self."[12] Unlike the buffered self, the porous self is under no illusions about its profound vulnerability in the face of innumerable influences, and these many influences blow through it like wind through curtains. You might say that, like curtains, the porous self dances and billows in response to the forces surrounding it. We find the sharpest embodiment of this mindset in the premodern world, where people saw themselves as inhabiting an enchanted universe filled with myriad unseen spiritual powers, some of them good, some of them wicked. Replace the modern fear of identity theft with demon possession and you're a step closer to the enchanted world of our distant forebears.[13]

But it wasn't all devils and possession. The physical world also seethed with a rich inner life. Gerard Manley Hopkins's celebrated excerpt from his poem "As Kingfishers catch fire, dragonflies draw flame," conveys a measure of this enchantment:

> Each mortal thing does one thing and the same;
> Deals out that being indoors each one dwells;
> Selves—goes itself; *myself* it speaks and spells,
> Crying *What I do is me: for that I came.*[14]

For Hopkins a tree in full bloom is exhibiting more than a natural life cycle; it is "selving," "dealing out that being indoors," and displaying the life God has endowed it with and which it is called to.

In this sense, nature doesn't reveal an impersonal inventory of "natural" processes. Rather, the created order reveals *mystery*—a word that's liable to mislead us modern, buffered types on two counts. On the one hand, we frequently see mystery as simply referring to something inscrutable or beyond explanation. People who use the word in this sense sound a lot like politicians who manage to sound profound when they're just being evasive. If, on the other hand, mystery signifies nothing more than a problem demanding a solution, like an elusive medical diagnosis or a detective story, we're still missing the full meaning. Mystery in the premodern sense does not reduce to a puzzle.

The theologian Hans Boersma says that for the premodern mind "'Mystery' referred to realities behind the appearances that one could observe by means of the senses. That is to say, though our hands, eyes, ears, nose, and tongue can access reality, they cannot *fully* grasp this reality. They cannot *comprehend* it."[15] That is, mystery in the full sense is neither merely elusive nor inscrutable; it is inexhaustible. God's world exceeds our full comprehension. Eustace Scrubb learns this lesson in C. S. Lewis's *Voyage of the Dawn Treader* when he tells Ramandu that in his world stars are "huge ball[s] of flaming gas." Ramandu—himself a former star—corrects him, "Even in your world, my son, that is not what a star is but only what it is made of."[16] The modern belief that material explanations exhaust the phenomena they describe, whether stars, plants, or persons, is as naive as it is typical.

Those who understand that they are porous recognize their susceptibility to these manifold influences. Here, many of us will automatically point to the dangers of superstition. After all, seeing a demon or a hobgoblin behind every rock and tree can put a damper on a person's social life. However, our naivety toward human frailty and vulnerability is a uniquely modern pathology that continues to wreak havoc in our households. The spell is so strong that it often takes a crisis to break it. Witness the fact that many of us don't realize how much we've been ignoring God until we come to a place where prayer is our last resort.

But no piece of technology punctures the convenient fantasy of the buffered self quite like our smartphones. The smartphone is, among other things, a portal into vast and unfathomable worlds—a kind of digital cosmos.[17] These worlds range from the uplifting to the amusing and all the way to the depraved and the demonic. Ironically, by showing us human vulnerability in the face of untold influences, our smartphones can help restore a measure of our lost enchantment. To be clear, we're not arguing for a superstitious fear of phones. We're using them to show that none of us live in buffered homes—that, like the people who inhabit them, our homes are always porous and permeable.

QUESTS WITHOUT A DESTINATION

Not everyone writes a memoir, but everyone has a story. If you've had the distinctly unflattering experience of stumbling across an old diary of yours, you'll probably agree that this is a good thing.

For all of its complexity, life consistently yields a narrative shape. Telling stories is thus our most profound means of making sense of our place in the world—a practice not unlike deciphering ancient cave paintings. As Roger Lundin observes, "Stories channel the aimless flow of time and turn our wanderings into quests."[18] We're all existential detectives trying to solve the riddle of our existence. It's one of the reasons that pastors, counselors, and spiritual directors are always on our case about keeping a journal. Our own stories are often so deeply internalized that we have to discover them before we can adequately express them. Before recitation, stories first require excavation.

But our stories are never just *our* stories; they're always shared. We are inescapably relational creatures. We don't just have a story;

we're part of a larger story, and this larger narrative unites us and defines the shape of our lives. Not only is this overarching story frequently unvoiced, but it's also often simply assumed. Generally speaking, the more oblivious we are to this story, the more powerful it is. Consequently, discovering this story is of the utmost importance for our households. If we want to address the many challenges in our homes, we need to begin by asking what story is defining them.

To get a handle on the story that shapes the lives of most Americans, think of the six abandoned characters in Luigi Pirandello's celebrated play *Six Characters in Search of an Author*. In the play the titular author withholds the one thing his characters most desire: "What was I denying them? Not themselves, clearly, but their drama, which interested them most."[19] Abandoned by their author, these six characters are dismayed to find themselves wandering into other plays in progress without a script or a guiding narrative. They are despairing, forlorn, and lost. It's a very un-American response.

In the "land of the free," we flaunt our authorlessness. We believe we choose our scripts and stories, and we like it that way. From Ralph Waldo Emerson's seminal essay "Self-Reliance" to Jack Kerouac's *On the Road*, the habit of waxing rhapsodic about the healing balm of restless self-determination goes to the very heart of the American imagination. Think of Emerson's searing words on the subject: "History is an impertinence and an injury, if it be any thing more than a cheerful apologue or parable of my being and becoming."[20] Whether we've read Emerson or not, we've all deeply internalized his message. It's a poetic description of our abiding conviction that freedom is synonymous with unrestricted choice and self-definition. From Caitlyn Jenner to Rachel Dolezal, Emerson's words continue to nourish our increasingly radical approaches to freedom and self-expression. In essence we believe that any limitation, be it geographical, ethnic, social, creedal, or biological, is "an impertinence and an injury."

It's fitting that former First Lady Michelle Obama chose *Becoming* as the title of her massively popular memoir. Her own words on the subject form an ideal complement to Emerson's musings: "For me, becoming isn't about arriving somewhere or achieving a certain aim. I see it instead as forward motion, a means of evolving, a way to reach continuously toward a better self."[21] Many Americans, whether we recognize it or not, are in hot pursuit of this ever-elusive "better self." Sometimes we think we'll find our better selves waiting for us at the end of the Appalachian Trail or a backpacking trip through Europe. Maybe a wine tour in France. Maybe a new house in a better, safer neighborhood. Maybe a new marriage or a new car. Maybe a new church. It's hard to say, but of one thing we're certain: we have to keep moving, evolving, *becoming*. The all-American story is a quest without a destination.

For many, Disneyland is still the "happiest place on earth" because it's more than an amusement park; it's a kingdom of endless possibilities, a bewitching haven in a world that feels more and more lifeless. For all its magical charms, though, it's highly revealing that Disney's Imagineers have yet to solve the riddle of Tomorrowland. Originally constructed in the 1950s, this section of the park is meant to dazzle us with a utopian vision of a distant future we can all eagerly anticipate.[22] But, as Walt Disney said himself, "The only problem with anything of tomorrow is that at the pace we're going right now, tomorrow would catch up with us before we got it built."[23]

With all due deference to Mr. Disney, there's a deeper problem. The all-American story doesn't include a destination. It's a vision that's never at rest. Disneyland itself may remain a dream destination for millions, but the failure of Tomorrowland offers a stark reminder that Americans still can't imagine much beyond the present.

Let's turn to one of America's premier theologians, Stanley Hauerwas, for a devastating but ultimately helpful diagnosis.

The narrative that you should have no story except the story you chose when you had no story obviously has implications for how faith is understood. It produces people who say things such as, "I believe Jesus is Lord—but that is just my personal opinion."[24] The grammar of this kind of avowal reveals a superficial person. But such people are the kind many think crucial for sustaining democracy. For to sustain a society that shares no goods in common other than the belief that there are no goods in common other than avoiding death, there must be people who will avoid any conflicts that might undermine the order, which is confused with peace. So an allegedly democratic society that styles itself as one made up of people of strong conviction becomes the most conformist of social orders, because of the necessity to avoid conflicts that cannot be resolved.[25]

If you're a Christian living in North America today, this is an uncompromising description of the spiritual location of your home. This is the story that's so deeply entrenched we have to speak it out loud to break its spell. Maybe you've had a professor inflict the celebrated philosopher and political theorist Thomas Hobbes on you. With his best-known work *Leviathan*, Hobbes achieved that most distinctive of literary honors: his name is now an adjective. When we want to describe any kind of ruthless, law-of-the-jungle environment, we can now call it "Hobbesian" because Hobbes argued that, in our natural state, we are radically free and fierce. Society therefore depends on the necessary evil of the law to constrain our unfettered freedom—otherwise, we'd all claw one another's eyes out.[26]

Most of us simply assume Hobbes's basic arguments. In the realm of pop culture think about how many of our postapocalyptic stories operate with a very simple and effective formula: subtract all modern technology and conveniences and watch the chaos ensue. But why is outright savagery a foregone conclusion in such circumstances? Even taking into account the pervasive issue of human corruption in all of its many forms, don't we also have ample evidence of people banding together in times of crisis? To be sure, Christianity makes it clear that human beings are fallen and thus predisposed to all manner of destructive behavior. But even so, the automatic assumption that we naturally revert to the laws of the jungle whenever the societal barriers are breached belies our deep-seated commitment to Hobbes's views of human nature.

Most of us think we chose our own stories. So let's have a quick look at some of the stories we tell about our lives and homes.

Many popular podcasts and television shows highlight our obsession with fraud and deception, but we don't need any famous impostors to put us on intimate terms with the gap between appearance and reality. Nowhere is this gap more apparent than in our homes, where we see and feel the awkward discrepancy between the stories we publish for the world and the brittle fragments of our actual lives. And, as we all know, the real story is often more Hieronymus Bosch than Thomas Kinkade.

In our increasingly disenchanted world, the word *story* still seems to hint at some hidden wholeness, some lost region where life is more than a monotony of scientific laws and static facts—a region where our lives make *sense*. Joan Didion famously said, "We tell ourselves stories in order to live."[27] Wrenched from its native context, this sentence might sound uplifting, but read Didion's full essay and you'll soon find that it's not meant to serve as an inspirational quote. Didion is reflecting on five particularly turbulent years—years in which her own basic sense of life's comprehensibility was unraveling. She makes clear that, in her view, any wholeness hinted at by stories is nothing more than a consoling myth, and her essay is getting at the artificial nature of the narratives we impose on the inherently formless shape of human experience. Imagine her response to our numerous "stories" on social media.

In many ways the desperate stories we tell on social media do confirm Didion's conviction. Much attention is paid to the amount of oversharing that takes place online. What is less noticed, however, is the subtle manner in which our various technologies enable an unprecedented level of secrecy. Social media provides us with a plethora of tools to carve away every unflattering pose, scar, and blemish. It's not just that our audience is seeing a carefully sculpted vision of our lives that bears little to no relation to our actual existence, but that we can communicate all of this on our terms, with none of the vulnerability that characterizes face-to-face interactions. It's never been easier to put a glossy finish on the chaos of our lives. Over and over again we shine our digital spotlights on our best moments while inwardly we're punctuated by increasing levels of distress. This is not story as an avenue onto a hidden wholeness or even a means of describing reality; this is story as a desperate coping mechanism for bringing together the disparate pieces of our lives. For Didion, storytellers are survivors, not poets.[28] Unlike most Americans, you might say that she is a character in search of an author. It's a step in the right direction.

CHRISTIAN HOMES AND THE CULTIVATION OF AN ETERNAL PERSPECTIVE

As a teenager Cameron experienced a good deal of cognitive dissonance when he read from authors like Joan Didion, William Faulkner, and Albert Camus. For all their pronounced differences, these writers all converge on the theme of humanity's essential lostness: Didion says that storytelling is a frantic coping mechanism. Faulkner channels Shakespeare to argue that life does indeed play out like "a tale told by an idiot full of sound and fury, signifying nothing." Camus compares our lives to the futile labor of Sisyphus, whose punishment from the gods is to perpetually push a stone up a hill, only to have it roll back down again. According to Camus, when your alarm goes off in the morning, you wrench yourself from the bed, and there sits your stone. His solution to this torturous existence? "We must imagine Sisyphus happy."[29] None of these writers would be surprised by the failures of Tomorrowland.

But if Christ is real, how can this be? Why do Didion, Faulkner, Camus, and so many others seem to be onto something when they imply that human life is hollow? If they're wrong, why do their stories resonate? For that matter, if the all-American story of Emerson and Michelle Obama is false, why does it ring true for so many of us?

As it happens, the book of Ecclesiastes has beat all of modernism's brooding existentialists and stoics to the punch line. In it Solomon shows that there are two broad ways of looking at life. On the one hand, there's the human perspective, which he designates "life under the sun." Its abiding feature is "vanity," which signifies the overall impermanence of all human aspirations. Think of Camus's stone waiting for you in the morning. But there is also the divine perspective, which regards the world from the standpoint of eternity. If we limit our gaze to life under the sun, it's clear that Didion is right: We eke out a meager existence and try to tell ourselves some consoling story about what it all means, when in fact it simply means nothing. Likewise, life under the sun isn't very kind to the vision of Tomorrowland. If we're true to the spirit of Solomon's portrayal of human endeavors, it's a safe bet that he might simply design Tomorrowland as a graveyard. After all, that's the one future destination we can all agree on. For all its implacable finality, death is remarkably nonpartisan.

Those who limit their gaze to life under the sun may appear to be grim realists. But they've fastened onto only one aspect of human experience. Andrew Delbanco, not a Christian himself, argues, "I stand by my claim that the most striking feature of contemporary culture is the unslaked craving for transcendence."[30] The preacher in Ecclesiastes simply says that God has set eternity in the hearts of humans (Ecclesiastes 3:11). The true realists therefore will not overlook the flattened dimensions of our modern, postindustrial world. But neither will they overlook our "unslaked craving for transcendence." The true realists will see life from an eternal perspective. This is a vision that's capacious enough to include all of the besetting limitations of life under the sun as well as the glories of a future designed not by an Imagineer but the author of our salvation. The true realists are therefore hopeful realists who can observe all of culture's seismic shifts with hearts animated by great expectations.

Unlike Americans, Christians are the ones who recognize their author, and their homes are defined by his story, rather than that of the surrounding culture. Roger Lundin conveys this story with majestic force.

> That the God of Abraham, that the force that rules the universe, that the power behind and beyond all events and all accidents, took on a body and became a child as fragile and delicate and vulnerable as this little one—this seems to me to be almost beyond imagining. But so it was, for the Word was made flesh and dwelt among us. And so it still is. And so it will forever be, throughout all ages, world without end.[31]

In Christ, we have an author, a story, and a destination. This book aims to describe households shaped by the true story of the Living God.

PART ONE

THREE COMMON MISCONCEPTIONS IN CHRISTIAN HOMES

1

FEAR PROTECTS

The Lord *is my light and my salvation;*
whom shall I fear?
The Lord *is the stronghold of my life;*
of whom shall I be afraid?

Psalm 27:1

We want to draw attention to one particular region within the Star Trek universe: the "neutral zone," a putatively safe space, which all galactic parties are obligated to honor. Of course, as the series unfolds, all kinds of covert operations, diabolical plots, and attempted surprise attacks occur in the neutral zone, reminding us that so-called neutral zones are not so neutral after all.

Sadly, a transcontinental flight is the closest most of us will get to an intergalactic voyage. But all of us crave safe spaces, and in our increasingly volatile cultural moment the idea of a neutral zone is appealing. For many of us the family home comes to mind. After all, this is our haven, the place in which to seek shelter and refuge from the wider world.

The problem comes when we seek a complete separation from the contaminating influences of daily life—a separation that remains practically unworkable. For many well-intentioned Christians who fear the degradation they perceive in our culture, the home becomes a kind of fortress—a place of isolation, a quarantined zone where bad ideas, images, and influences are held at bay and kept out of the range of infection. For some the protective measures go well beyond the censure of pop culture. If you've encountered the strange world of preppers—a contemporary permutation of the survivalism of the atomic age—you've likely seen an interior-decorating scheme that has more in common with a bunker than a home.

Of course, we do need to build safe spaces, and the home should be a place where we instruct our kids, protect our families, and nurture our values. But we cannot be naive about how influences penetrate both hearts and homes. Our homes are always porous and permeable, and they inevitably display some culture or other, whether we like it or not. The influence of media has been vastly amplified in recent years and there is simply no way to seal off minds and hearts from exposure to the wider world.

Smartphones may be new, but the challenge of being a faithful witness in a world that's actively hostile to the gospel is a perennial feature of the Christian life. It's also a task we're called to enter into with love, humility, and joy—not fear, paranoia, and suspicion. One of this book's main contentions is that Christians ought to cultivate discernment in place of fear. We don't want to be naive about the state of the world around us, but neither do we want to see ourselves as somehow immune to it either. Rather, we want to gain the eternal perspective that helps to make sense of the world as it is and is it will one day be.

THREE HARMFUL BYPRODUCTS OF THE
FEAR-PROTECTS MINDSET

Marilynne Robinson has a two-tier thesis about contemporary America: First, it is full of fear. "And second, fear is not a Christian habit of mind."[1] For all America's deep divisions, fear remains a nonpartisan phenomenon, a sad point of unity in our national life. It's not just the nonstop headlines of shootings, police brutality, the immigration crisis, and growing civil unrest. It's that all of these tragic events only spark more division and acrimony in their wake. Mass shootings, for instance, have become a kind of sickening new normal, and every time one of these atrocities is carried out it rehashes a vicious public debate that grows increasingly politicized. In such a context true mourning and reckoning are all but impossible. Both sides of the political aisle are characterized by mutual bad faith, and everyone seems convinced of the pernicious motives of her ideological neighbor. This is the world we send our children into. Little wonder we've grown overprotective.

Though the apostle Peter calls us "resident aliens" because we won't reach our true home until we are face-to-face with our Lord, it's difficult to strike the balance of being "in the world but not of it," and we're often tempted to gravitate toward one of the twin extremes of cultural isolation and assimilation. Ideally, this tension enables us to strike the proper balance: to invest in our world while maintaining an eternal perspective that qualifies all our human endeavors. Successes can be celebrated and failures can be mourned, but neither calcifies into the type of worldliness that keeps us from God's kingdom.

But a crude reading of the "in and not of" tension can also lead to a mindset that we're calling "fear protects." The fear-protects mindset views the world outside the church as so thoroughly compromised that anything more than a modest level of engagement risks contamination. It fosters a highly insular way of life that seeks to build a wholesome counterculture of alternative institutions for the education and nourishment of its members. Though not always a direct byproduct of this line of thinking, fear protects includes everything from homeschooling

and Christian higher education to church camps and youth retreats to the Christianized counterparts to Hollywood movies
and alternative music.

Speaking specifically of fear protects, we'd like to explore three
harmful habits of mind—namely, dualism, spiritual elitism, and
the glamorization of the forbidden.

In the early days after his conversion, Stuart learned firsthand
about the pitfalls of dualism. At that time he viewed anything
that was not explicitly Christian as either inherently evil or as a
real threat to the spiritual life. Most of the books on holiness he
was reading defined the Christian life primarily in oppositional
terms, pitting the church against the world. This is not entirely
unwarranted—after all, Christians ought to resist anything that
undermines Christ's authority. Consequently, there's a principled
abstemiousness in the lives of Christian men and women, which
will strike some as prudishness. But Stuart's resistance went
beyond prudence. His worldview began with giving primacy of
place to the fall and sin.

Stuart's overestimation of darkness led him to underestimate
the goodness of God's creation, the significance of the creation
mandate, and the ultimate act of divine affirmation, namely,
Christ's incarnation. This imbalance is a mark of immature faith.
God's Word doesn't see the world as a spiritual desert marked by
the Lord's disapproving absence. Instead, Scripture is filled with
imagery extolling the virtues of God's creation. Psalm 19:1 exclaims,
"The heavens declare the glory of God, and the sky above proclaims
his handiwork." Proverbs 3:19-20 spells out creation's legibility in
terms of wisdom and knowledge:

> The LORD by wisdom founded the earth;
>> by understanding he established the heavens;
> by his knowledge the deeps broke open,
>> and the clouds drop down the dew.

Christians down the ages have celebrated this abundant comprehensibility as God's wisdom. And the natural sciences continue to disclose the creative scope of his wisdom. Offering a poetic summary of the many prophetic celebrations of God's creative wisdom, the apostle Paul declares that in Christ "all things hold together" (Colossians 1:17).

By downplaying the significance of the created order, Stuart had mistakenly given more authority to the devil than was his due and had failed to distinguish legitimate goods from damaged and corrupted ones. He had misunderstood God's gifts in creation and the role of pleasure in experiencing his good provisions. In his zeal Stuart had unconsciously assigned all that seemed to bring physical or cultural pleasure to the domain of darkness. During those early days, he viewed most cultural productions (especially movies and music) as dangerous. Not even literary geniuses were exempt. Early in his relationship with his soon-to-be wife, Stuart expressed stern disapproval at her reading of Irving Stone's *The Agony and the Ecstasy*.

So just how does this mindset lead to dualism? In effect, casting such a withering gaze on the earthly aspects of life largely evicts Christ from its daily precincts. Sociologists and philosophers often spell this out in terms of a sacred-secular divide, but practically it tends to keep Christ in churches and religious gatherings and out of the fine texture of day-to-day living. You leave the service, prayer meeting, conference, or retreat and head back into the "real world." Our spiritual lives are highly prized, while the quotidian obstacle course of dirty diapers, leaking gutters, and check engine lights is seen as mundane chores at best, a profane test of endurance at worst.

We stated in the introduction that many so-called Christian homes mirror the surrounding culture in ways they don't even recognize, and here we find a powerful example. At this juncture we need to briefly nod in the direction of ancient dualisms to flesh out the modern translation in our homes. Speaking broadly, each of these dualisms regards the physical world as inherently inferior to the spiritual one. From Manichaeism to Gnosticism, the principled condemnation of the created order tends to terminate in one of two extremes: asceticism and hedonism. If you think the world is a thoroughly contaminated realm of darkness that militates against the soul, you may express your contempt through either self-denial or overindulgence. Asceticism expresses its hostility through antagonism: if the world is defiled, I want nothing to do with it. Hedonism expresses its disdain through apathy: if the world (including my physical body) is defiled, nothing I do matters. My soul remains intact as my flesh pursues its degrading hobbies.

Homes shaped by dualism blaze a middle path between the extremes of asceticism and hedonism. For instance, Stuart expressed his contempt for the world through his resistance to the wider culture. He purged his massive record collection, turned his nose up at all "secular entertainment," and read only Christian literature. However, this kind of asceticism is usually counterbalanced by a principled apathy regarding the created order. This is where we encounter pronounced irresponsibility in everything from diet to environmental concerns. When Cameron moved from Europe to the United States in the late 1990s, for instance, he began to notice an odd imbalance in many of the Christian homes in the Bible Belt South. While there would be a laudable emphasis on understanding Scripture and the Christian worldview, there was consistent neglect in the realms of diet and rest. The assumption wasn't so much that overindulgence and overwork were beneficial habits as it was that care for one's body was an expendable part of the Christian life. Pressing into the matter, Cameron was surprised to discover that wholesome eating and regular exercise were often regarded as distractions to one's devotion. Though this may seem harmless enough, it can amount to dismissing the body as little more than an inferior part of the physical world, a view utterly foreign to the Christian faith, which turns on the physical resurrection of its Lord and Savior and promises a resurrected body to each of his followers. If, however, the world is viewed as thoroughly compromised, it's easy to forget that all things hold together in Christ. Indeed, it becomes easier and easier to live as though he doesn't exist.

Stuart's aversion to Irving Stone and his old record collection was an unwitting division of the sacred from the secular, the public from the private, and faith from reason. It neatly divided Christianity from the rest of life. In our devotion to Christianity we need to guard against the tendency to elevate it into irrelevance. If Christ dwells exclusively on the mountaintops, he'll play little to no role in our daily lives. For this reason many well-intentioned men and women cultivate homes marked by his absence rather than his active presence. When Cameron and his sister would leave the house to catch the bus for high school, their mom used to tell them, "Remember the Lord!" It sounded hokey to Cameron, but it turned out to be a needed prophetic word because, though he wouldn't have articulated it like this at the time, his tacit assumption was often that God wouldn't deign to show up in a place as spiritually sterile as a public high school. By challenging the lie that the Lord is too holy for daily life, Mary reaffirmed his inescapable presence. We would all do well to go about our daily tasks with the phrase "Remember the Lord!" ringing in our ears.

The dualism that slowly degenerates into a form of unwitting atheism is subtle. Spiritual elitism, on the other hand, is much more in-your-face. If we inculcate the fear-protects mindset in our households, we are liable to foster deep hostility for those we view as threats. In this sense, fear is a recipe for an us-and-them ap-proach to the world. While it's vital to have spaces that provide shelter and rest from the world, we need to guard against the tendency to allow fear to lead us into spiritual elitism. Consequently, any form of strategic cultural retreat must never fall prey to this us-and-them dynamic. To do so would be more than arrogant; it would be downright naive. Whatever shape the center of cultural retreat takes, it won't be exempt from the challenges posed by fallen human nature. After all, if Christianity is true, we are all part of the problem. In this sense there's an inherently self-congratulatory aspect to the ubiquitous statements about our nation's precipitous cultural decline. If the culture is in decline, we're certainly numbered in that decline.

One of the best ways to puncture our sense of self-righteousness is to do the hard work seeing those with whom we have deep disagreements as human beings. Drawing from cultural anthropology, Alan Jacobs introduces us to an arresting phrase: "repugnant cultural other" (RCO).[2] An RCO is more than your ideological opponent; it's the person you're tempted to call evil, the person who occupies all of the positions you believe to be the most harmful. Whether we want to admit it or not, all of us have an RCO. Here's a good litmus test: if you consider a basic concession to the common humanity of a certain person to be a form of treason or compromise, you've got your RCO. Needless to say, said person frequently holds some form of political office. If you're a Christian, however, your RCO is more than a fellow human being; they are your neighbor. When Christ put the words *good* and *Samaritan* together for his Jewish audience, he knew what he was doing (Luke 10:25-37). By equating the RCO of his listeners with their neighbor, Jesus was giving a firm rebuke to their deep-seated prejudice. In our day, many of us need to hear phrases like "the good Republican," "the good Democrat," "the good social justice warrior," "the good Muslim," and "the good Hindu," to feel the full prophetic force of our Lord's words.

Jonathan Haidt and Greg Lukianoff identify the notion that "life is a battle between good people and evil people" as one of the great untruths of our age because it conveniently takes us off the hook and effectively justifies any measures we take against those we deem evil.[3] Interestingly, neither Haidt nor Lukianoff is a Christian—Haidt is himself a thoroughgoing naturalist. Given Christ's words on the matter, however, Christians can go further and declare that this untruth is both idolatrous and hateful. It's idolatrous because it elevates us above the common fray of humanity, and it's hateful because it conveniently justifies our vilification of others. This mindset generates RCOs, not neighbors. It is indeed a thoroughly un-Christian habit of mind. The sad irony is that if our homes are characterized by suspicion, fear, and paranoia, they are mirroring the surrounding culture, not challenging it.

The final harmful byproduct of the fear-protects mindset is the glamorization of the forbidden. Though the phrase may sound a bit cumbersome, it simply refers to the well-known fact that when something is declared off-limits it instantly becomes more appealing. When Cameron and his wife, Heather, were navigating the toddler years with their son, for instance, they quickly learned that sentences beginning with "don't" were not nearly as effective as those that began by offering an alternative: "Look at *this*." From our earliest years we are incorrigible trespassers. In the words of Chaucer's Wife of Bath: "Forbid us thing, and that desire we."[4]

It's important to stress that we're using the term *forbidden* and not *evil*. Christians recognize that we live in a fallen world, but we also acknowledge that God's grace shines through in surprising places. It's one of the reasons the apostle Paul is able to shed light on the gospel by quoting from pagan poets in Acts 17. Numerous Christians continue to follow Paul's example by drawing on everyone from poets to directors to songwriters to skeptical philosophers. We'll explore Paul's strategy in greater detail in a later chapter—for now, it's worth noting that Paul is not necessarily being prescriptive in his use of these two non-Christian voices. We can applaud his creative approach to evangelism while recognizing that he's not enjoining all of us to read Aratus and Miletus.

In fact, given Paul's clear teaching on anything that constitutes a hindrance to someone else's faith, he would have conceivably placed these two poets off-limits to plenty of folks in his day in much the same way that we would with our contemporary poets, be they actual poets or filmmakers, novelists, or musicians. Paul can draw on these artists in the rarified atmosphere of the Areopagus, but they don't make an appearance in any of his epistles. Likewise, the fact that your pastor may glean some theological insights from David Fincher's *Seven* doesn't mean that he's instructing you to drop everything you're doing and immediately screen the film. As we think about the boundaries and restrictions in our own homes, let's keep in mind that they're not necessarily binding on everyone. Different temperaments, sensibilities, and sensitivities are important factors where cultural artifacts are concerned. Though the fear-protects mindset often oversimplifies things by issuing a sweeping condemnation, Scripture paints a more complex picture of our cultural landscape.

That said, we all know restrictions cast a powerful spell over everything they touch. Declare something off-limits and it's like waving a magic wand that instantly provokes desire. Remember the marketing campaigns behind old horror films? "Do you have a weak heart?" "A weak constitution?" "Are you easily shocked?" "If so, avoid this film!" The fact that this is just garden-variety reverse psychology does little to undermine its effectiveness.

From Pandora to Prometheus we know that our curiosity about anything forbidden is as powerful as it is insatiable. But the most incisive voice on the matter belongs to the serpent in the Garden of Eden: "God knows that when you eat of it your eyes will be opened, and you will be like God, knowing good and evil" (Genesis 3:5). Eve bites into the forbidden fruit because she's lured by the promise of secret knowledge that will make her "like God." This satanic invitation has lost none of its appeal in our day: we remain a race of incorrigible rebels. Our penchant for playing God continually inspires us to transgress all boundaries and push human experience to the furthest frontiers in every arena, from sexuality to science.

Since fear protects tends to cast the outside world in almost exclusively forbidden terms, the outside world often takes on an enchanting aspect, particularly for the adolescent members of the home. Growing up in the cloistered environment of the mission field, Cameron well remembers this culture of deep anxiety regarding anything outside the church. On one occasion he was spending the night with a friend. They were talking in his room and without thinking, Cameron turned on a CD he'd brought along. Instantly, his friend's dad popped his head in and pointed to the stereo. "Is that Christian?" Blinking, Cameron responded, "No." His friend's dad wrinkled his nose in distaste. "Turn it *off*."

This is not to say kids should get carte blanche on all cultural engagement. Parents are responsible for guiding the young hearts and minds in their homes, and each child is unique in their sensibilities and sensitivities. Rather, what we want to highlight here is a kneejerk reaction that frequently backfires. There's a fine line between establishing wholesome boundaries and a self-nullifying spiritual paranoia that undermines itself by imbuing forbidden objects with outsized power. In this case, by overestimating the power of a particular song—the work of a decidedly mediocre rock band hardly worthy of the compliment, by the way—this dad greatly enhanced its appeal. Cynical marketers know that scaring parents is an effective way to sell records.

There's nothing wrong with asking someone to turn off a song that violates the standards of your home, but treating it like some kind of cursed object that defiles whatever it touches is a way of thinking that shares more in common with animism than with Christianity. While we don't want to underestimate the power of harmful influences, we don't want to overestimate them either. Given that anything forbidden exerts a powerful and primal pull on all of us, we need to avoid any kind of reaction that intensifies the appeal. Though there's no one-size-fits-all formula for such an undertaking, we can begin by establishing a precedent of exercising healthy caution and parental authority in place of fear and control.

RECOVERING THE FEAR OF THE LORD

What role does fear play in your home? The fear of losing one's faith or of our kids losing theirs; the fear of contamination from bad or impure ideas; the fear of bowing to cultural trends and priorities. These are not matters to be taken lightly. Discernment ought to replace our habitual fear of the surrounding world. We'd like to draw attention to an important distinction that Stuart encountered in his early years. Deeply immersed in the tension of being in the world but not of it, he came across the words of Richard John Neuhaus, who proposed that as Christians we are "in the world and not of the world," but also "*for* the world."

Fear need not guide us. We choose faith and hope as we live in love. We face life's many challenges with seriousness and practicality, but we also know the liberty of casting our cares on the one who forms our hearts and shepherds our homes. In sharp contrast to our culture's chronic anxiety, Scripture extols the fear of the Lord: "The fear of the LORD is the beginning of knowledge; fools despise wisdom and instruction" (Proverbs 1:7).

The Christian view of reality is rooted in our understanding of the sovereign God who is the creator and the sustainer of all—the one in whom "all things hold together." The psalmist tells us "our times are in His hands" (Psalm 31:15) and that he is our light, so "whom should we fear?" (Psalm 27:1). As Jesus was about to ascend to the Father, he promised the disciples that he would be with them always. This promise of his presence is an anchor for our souls because it reminds us that there is no place where we can escape the Lord's presence. If you truly believe that Christ is with you in every circumstance of your life and that he alone sustains you, fear cannot control you. The biblical narrative, with all its hardships, sufferings, and glory, reminds us that we do indeed live in a fallen world. But it also tells of the risen Savior who is soon returning to make all things new. For this reason, Christians are in the world, and not of it—but also *for* it.

2

INFORMATION SAVES

For this reason I bow my knees before the Father, from whom
every family in heaven and on earth is named, that according
to the riches of his glory he may grant you to be strengthened
with power through his Spirit in your inner being, so that
Christ may dwell in your hearts through faith—that you, being
rooted and grounded in love, may have strength to comprehend
with all the saints what is the breadth and length and height
and depth, and to know the love of Christ that surpasses
knowledge, that you may be filled with all the fullness of God.

Nothing will teach you about your mechanical ineptitude quite like buying a new house. This was Cameron's unfortunate discovery as he began to explore the dustier recesses of his new home. Exhibit A: The decrepit toilet in the master bathroom requiring immediate replacement. One text later and a trusted friend showed up with a box full of exotic tools that may as well have been torture devices for all Cameron knew. "It's really pretty simple," said the friend as, wielding a wrench, he performed an operation that seemed a stone's throw away from nuclear fusion or brain surgery. Cameron "helped" by handing tools to his friend and holding the new commode in place as it was painstakingly lowered onto its rim of fresh beeswax.

Despite the advice of friends and family to simply consult the plethora of YouTube tutorials, Cameron's attempts at DIY solutions to basic home projects remain abject failures. Why? The question is deceptively simple. With our unfettered access to reams and reams of information, shouldn't we be able to solve most of our problems? Shouldn't expertise be obsolete or, at the very least, as common as free Wi-Fi access? And shouldn't Cameron be able to do much more than hand tools to a friend? Shouldn't he be able to, say, add a new wing onto his home?

We need a philosopher to tell us about the limitations of those YouTube videos. Specifically, we need the help of Hungarian polymath Michael Polanyi. Polanyi's day job was as a chemist, but his lasting contributions are in the field of epistemology—a hideous word for the formal study of knowledge that promptly scares away most nonacademics. In truth, this field is deeply practical; it seeks to understand how we know what we know.

Polanyi is particularly concerned with all of our knowledge that evades precise description or articulation. In his own words his project takes shape by "starting from the fact that *we can know more than we can tell.*"[1] Take, for example, the fact that most of us are much better at *recognizing* faces than we are at *describing* them. Guiding the artistic vision of a police sketch artist is much more challenging than picking out a face in a police lineup. Try describing a friend's face without looking at any images or photos and you'll have a feel for this confounding rift between what we can know and say. Many of us experience a similar confusion when we're asked to say passwords out loud, give detailed directions to a familiar destination, or offer clear verbal instructions for a family recipe that's as old as your mom's faded oven mitt.

But it's not just that we know more than we can say. Some of the most breathtaking feats of human skill and ingenuity, whether they involve paints, power tools, athletic gear, or musical instruments, seem utterly beyond the reach of words. This certainly seems to be the case when world-class athletes try to explain their dazzling performances. David Foster Wallace offers a striking example in his review of tennis prodigy Tracy Austin's sports memoir, *Beyond Center Court*, a book that purports to give its readers an intimate tour of what it's like to be in the kind of mental zone that most of us can only dream about. According to Wallace,

> Explicitly or not, the memoirs make a promise—to let us penetrate the indefinable mystery of what makes some persons geniuses, semidivine, to share with us the secret and so both to reveal the difference between us and them and to erase it, a little, that difference . . . to give us the (we want, expect, only one, the master narrative, the key) Story.[2]

But the sad truth is that "great athletes usually turn out to be stunningly inarticulate about those qualities and experiences that constitute their fascination."[3] Polanyi may be philosophically dense, but he's one of the few people who can deliver on Tracy Austin's promises and unlock the hidden dimensions of her skill and ingenuity. Unlike Wallace, he doesn't need an inane sports memoir to confirm that someone like Austin knows much more than she can say. In our era of social media scrutiny and instant celebrity access, many of us experience daily the marked discrepancy between brilliant performances and "stunningly inarticulate" performers who should probably have their phones confiscated by their publicists.

The people who make how-to videos on YouTube may not be decorated athletes, but they still know more than they can say. What remains unseen and largely unsayable, of course, is the intense regimen of practice and habit formation that requires these people to submit as apprentices to the authority of a trusted master, and to learn by example. In a word, what lies behind their prowess is a *tradition*.

In his perceptive profile of *Parts Unknown* host and celebrity chef Anthony Bourdain, Patrick Radden Keefe points to the stabilizing role of the tradition of jujitsu in Bourdain's nomadic existence: "He had always loved the kitchen because it was a tribe, and in jujitsu he had found another sweaty, grueling activity with its own hierarchy and lingo, a vocabulary of signs and symbols that would be impossible for an outsider to understand."[4] It's impossible for an outsider to understand because the only way to fully comprehend it is to submit to its traditions—the legacy of habits and signs that have been passed down through the ages. It's the reason that Bourdain could step onto mats all around the globe with perfect strangers, enter into the visceral intimacy of physical combat, and still feel a bond that withstands all social and cultural boundaries. You might say that jujitsu was his church.

Polanyi's description deftly captures the hidden dynamics of a tradition,

> To learn by example is to submit to authority. You follow your master because you trust his manner of doing things even when you cannot analyze and account in detail for its effectiveness. By watching the master and emulating his efforts in the presence of his example, the apprentice *unconsciously picks up the rules of the art*, including those which are not explicitly known to the master himself. These hidden rules can be assimilated only by a person who surrenders himself to that extent uncritically to the imitation of another.[5]

Cameron's friend's seemingly effortless hammer swings were preceded by numerous other hammer swings, many of them inaccurate and clumsy. The grueling day-in and day-out of constant practice brought the needed refinement to his motions. He was born into a family and a community with a legacy of skilled craftsmanship, and this rich tapestry is part of the invisible force behind his enviable proficiency with tools—part of the reason he's "good with his hands"—another infuriatingly simple phrase that's about as helpful as the star athlete's "I just got out there and did my best." By watching his dad (the master craftsman) and then making the slow trek from theory and observation to practice, he was able to develop a skill that remains as useful as it is inscrutable. While he can offer a set of rigid instructions on replacing a toilet, he can't distill an entire tradition into discreet chunks of information. Nobody can. For the most part, YouTube handymen and women are speaking to people within their tradition. Naturally, there are varying levels of experience and skill among their audience members, but they're still speaking to the initiated—to people with callused hands. Lacking his friend's rich tradition, Cameron gleans mostly static information from these videos. True, he can learn, but he'll need more than information to do so. He'll need a master and a tradition.

Nevertheless, many Christian parents believe those YouTube videos are enough. That is, they believe that information alone can secure the stability of their kids' faith. We're calling this misconception the "information saves" mindset, and the thinking goes something like this: if we do all that we can to ensure that our children have all the necessary information about Christianity, then the rest of their lives will fall into place. They will be able to answer their atheist professor's loud objections to their faith. They will resist the manifold temptations that come their way. They will get plugged in to the right churches, and they will *stay* in those churches.

But information alone, no matter how accurate and precise, can no more form Christian disciples than YouTube tutorials can form carpenters. And the missing pieces are the same: the master and the tradition. Christians who wish to give nothing more than intellectual lip service to Christ are a bit like musicians who only read sheet music but refuse to play any actual instruments. From carpentry to Christianity, education is always an expansive endeavor, one that involves the whole person. It always moves beyond theory to practice.

James K. A. Smith sounds a lot like Polanyi in his helpful overview: "An education, then, is a constellation of practices, rituals, and routines that inculcates a particular vision of the good life by inscribing or infusing that vision into the heart (the gut) by means of material, embodied practices."[6] Joining your dad in the kitchen to learn the subtleties of a cherished family recipe, shuffling forward on your march to take Communion on a Sunday morning, practicing a song on the piano until its melody is practically part of your DNA, experiencing your child's baptism: these are all embodied practices that aptly demonstrate that learning goes way beyond the mastery of information. Along with his wedding, Cameron counts the blinking look of astonishment on his children's faces as the baptismal waters touched their heads as the most beautiful moments of his life, and, as any parent in this position will tell you, the experience is much more than intellectual.

And yet many parents continue to believe that the longevity of their child's faith depends on the right books, curriculums, conferences, or podcasts. One well-meaning mother recently told us that her teenage son gets to enjoy a litany of "edifying" podcasts whenever he's a passenger in her car. "Teachable moments with my captive audience," as she says. We're not disparaging any of these resources, of course. Used properly, they can help to cultivate a more robust understanding of the Christian worldview. When they're seen as ends rather than means, however, these same tools can become distractions at best, obstacles at worst. After some conversations with this lady's son it quickly became apparent that he had zero interest in any of these extensive podcasts, and that he regarded the lengthy excursions with mom as nothing more than a teeth-gritting test of endurance. Needless to say, this captive audience member wasn't taking any notes.

In this sense many Christian parents implicitly disagree with Blaise Pascal's famous dictum that the "heart has its reasons of which reason knows nothing." Instead, they opt to prioritize mind over heart.[7] Despite its fame, Pascal's quote doesn't take care of itself. Without context it seems to be an eloquent expression of the law of most Disney movies—namely, "follow your heart." Pascal is wiser than that, though, and the philosopher Peter Kreeft can help us to see the profundity of his holistic understanding of the heart:

> We all know that a friend who loves you deeply *knows* you more adequately than a scientist who only studies you as a specimen. A psychologist is someone who knows *about* you; a friend is someone who *knows* you. Other languages than English make this clear: the distinction between *wissen* and *kennen* in German, *savoir* and *connaître* in French.[8]

How many of our kids know all *about* Christianity but don't know Christ? As Pascal has it, the vision of the heart is not unlike the knowing glance of a trusted friend. This is knowledge by acquaintance rather than mere propositional knowledge. The only way to truly know anything or anyone is to move beyond description to an experiential level.

Think of the awkward social dance that starts at the beginning of a friendship. There's a reason so many comedies, romantic and otherwise, zero in on the clumsy motions of this dance. Our faltering steps toward intimacy are as funny as they are touching. Let's call this clumsy back and forth *the friendship dance*. The friendship dance is all about the things we love rather than our intellectual commitments. We're much more likely to ask our new dance partner about what they like doing (eating, listening, watching, etc.) because we instinctively know that their habits, hobbies, and routines will tell us all about who they are. A sociologist will hand you a survey, but someone trying to get to know you will ask you about which songs you jam out to in the car while you're heading to your favorite coffee shop. Practically speaking, if you want to do anything with someone else, you have to locate common interests. If you hate disc golf, for instance (guilty), that may pull you off the dance floor with certain folks before the friendship can even get started.

There's a very real sense in which someone's love of fly-fishing or *Dungeons and Dragons* will tell you more about who they are than a survey of their supposed intellectual commitments ever will. People will offer all sorts of knowledgeable advice on healthy eating habits, for instance, but if you want to know what they think, take a look in their fridge. A key aspect of the Christian life involves bridging the gap between the head and the heart. Mere information can't perform the vital service of reforming our desires, of bringing us to the place where our desires match our virtues. James K. A. Smith says,

> Being a disciple of Jesus is not primarily a matter of getting the right ideas and doctrines and beliefs into your head in order to guarantee proper behavior; rather, it's a matter of being the kind of person who *loves* rightly—who loves God and neighbor and is oriented to the world by the primacy of that love.[9]

We cannot love anything rightly unless we move beyond mere information. Cameron can watch all the online tutorials he wants, but until he picks up a hammer and develops some calluses of his own, his knowledge will remain purely theoretical. Information is necessary but not sufficient. Similarly, if Christian parents want to help cultivate spiritual maturity in their children, they need to do much more than instill correct thinking; they need to introduce their children to the Master and the tradition—to Christ and his church.

3

SPIRITUAL EDUCATION BELONGS TO EXPERTS

Calling to him a child, he put him in the midst of them and said, "Truly, I say to you, unless you turn and become like children, you will never enter the kingdom of heaven."

MATTHEW 18:2-3

In our work as apologists, we encounter a consistent mindset among parents who are deeply concerned about the spiritual well-being of their children. Though each situation is unique and often complex, the basic request can be summed up with a simple phrase: "Fix my kid!"

To honor these moms and dads, we're going to make a careful distinction between their good intentions and a deeply entrenched mindset that's as prevalent as it is misguided. The mindset in question is a cultural byproduct of what French philosopher Jacques Ellul calls "technique"—the modern obsession with securing total control with maximum efficiency. This thinking shows up in several contemporary phrases, all of which center on some form of technical mastery or optimization. "Life hack," "because science," "living my best life," and the faintly sinister "killing it" are just a few of technique's colloquial expressions. But this worldview has also come to dominate many of our daily habits. We've got apps designed to increase our productivity by counting down the days of our lives; we've got meal-replacement drinks so we don't have to waste time preparing and sharing food with fellow humans; we've even got features that help us speed up our podcasts so we can plow through reams of content more efficiently.

As Ellul points out, the price of this relentless drive for efficiency is a growing sense of dehumanization. Architecture that prioritizes function over form also helps us picture technique. From the alien vistas of the modern city's monolithic skyscrapers to the barren nightmare of wartime bunkers to the mechanized horrors of the labor camp that effectively converts its prisoners into biological machinery, technique works by reducing everyone and everything to a problem awaiting a technical solution.

With the best of intentions, many parents follow this line of thinking to their kids. By reducing a child to little more than a solvable problem, these parents' request to "Fix my kid!" fits neatly into Ellul's category and caters to the notion that moms and dads are essentially parental engineers seeking technical solutions for their kid's problems. It's easy to see how this ambition follows close on the heels of the information-saves mindset. We want to secure the correct information for the optimal functioning of our convictions. It's simply a matter of plugging in to the right channels. Recall the mom who subjected her son to hours of "edifying" podcasts in the hope of rejuvenating his spiritual life. It's tempting to speculate that she sped these programs up for maximum efficiency.

Christianity can't be downloaded. Though there's no shortage of Bible apps and subcultural algorithms from the world of evangelicalism, there is no Christian life hack that will help you *kill it* in your devotional life. The parents who approach us at conferences and youth events have discovered this firsthand. Sadly, they often draw the wrong conclusion from their experiences.

OUTSOURCING THE "PROBLEM"

Not long ago Cameron was part of a youth conference with an undeniably strained dynamic. The speakers radiated the usual energy and enthusiasm that characterizes these events. Their young audience, however, sat in stolid silence, defensively brandishing their phones. Most of the kids had zero interest in being there. Finally, the emcee asked them to raise their hands if a parent had forced them to attend. Nearly every hand in the auditorium shot up. *Fix my kid!* echoed in Cameron's mind as he scanned the crowd in that dimly lit room.

The whole thing put him in mind of some of his classmates from his Bible college days. Desperate parents frequently see Christian colleges as a kind of spiritual military school, and they lean heavily on the faculty and administration to reform their kids. Ironically, this benevolent form of coercion only serves to undermine parental authority. During a particularly contentious disagreement in his teenage years, Cameron's mother said, "One day you'll discover firsthand just how hard parenting is. The world can be a terrible place, and nobody prepares you for the dilemmas you'll face." She didn't realize it at the time, but this haunting insight pierced straight through her son's defensive armor. Make no mistake, parenting is hard and the temptation to lean on someone who claims to have all the answers is often motivated by increasing levels of desperation. Nevertheless, it amounts to an abdication of parental responsibility. Here we arrive at our final common misconception: *spiritual education belongs to experts.*

Before proceeding, we want to be clear that we're not disparaging any of the resources available to Christian families. We wouldn't be writing this book if that were the case. From podcasts to conferences to youth leaders to books and training seminars, the church offers an embarrassment of riches for families. Though we're not denigrating these efforts, we *are* arguing that they can't take the place of parenting. A child's spiritual education is the primary responsibility of their mom and dad. We're also going to join with responsible clergy and theologians worldwide in arguing that there are no spiritual experts. Longtime pastor and theologian Harold Senkbeil brings a wealth of experience to his work as a minister, having pastored everywhere from rural to urban settings and having taught in seminaries as well as playing a leading role in a parachurch ministry that trains pastors. Nevertheless, this seasoned minister maintains, "Frankly, if you run into someone who claims to be an expert at ministry, you should run the other way."[1] Amplifying this claim, he argues, "We can't apply a spiritual stethoscope or blood pressure monitor to the soul; only God himself sees into the human heart. So spiritual ministry by definition can't be measured."[2] Though Senkbeil has pastors in mind here, we can apply his observations to parents as well. Because God alone sees our children's hearts, we can soundly conclude that no so-called expert can fix or solve them.

Of course, this doesn't stop many parents from continuing to see those in frontline ministry (especially pastors) as a species of professional Christian. Though the classic vocation of pastors is soul care, the idea that they can subject the human spirit to the same kind of conclusive analysis as an x-ray or a blood test is a notion utterly foreign to Christianity. This line of thinking places prayer and urinalysis on roughly equal footing. It's a simple but profound category mistake, one that brings us to a greatly misunderstood and much-needed word.

Mystery is perhaps one of the more misunderstood words nowadays (though *paradox* is up there too). It's often the place we retreat to when we're out of ideas but still want to sound profound. Many conversations have stalled at the impasse of mystery. "The Lord works in mysterious ways" may well be one of the most infamous of Christian bromides. The word *mystery* also strikes a disingenuous note since it can give the impression that its user has gained access to hidden realms beyond the reach of ordinary mortals.

Theologian Hans Boersma helps us to recover a more holistic understanding of this vexed word. In the biblical sense a mystery is neither solvable nor inscrutable. Rather, it is something that *exceeds* our full comprehension.[3] Think of the countless books devoted to the subject of Christ's incarnation. Scores of brilliant and highly articulate scholars discuss the matter on a routine basis in both formal and informal settings. Despite the plethora of insight, no one will ever fully wrap their mind around the fact that Christ is "very God and very man." Christ's incarnation remains a mystery not because it's inscrutable but because it's inexhaustible.

Though human beings don't share in Christ's divinity, we remain mysteries to ourselves as well. The church father Gregory of Nyssa even goes so far as to defend divine mystery by pointing to our inability to comprehend ourselves: "I also ask: Who has known his own mind? Those who think themselves capable of grasping the nature of God would do well to consider whether they have looked into themselves."[4] (It goes without saying that this insight applies to our current obsession with personality tests.) But why are human beings mysteries? Isn't this just another clever rhetorical ploy to help us avoid a more responsible conversation? Peter Kreeft explores mystery as a "'problem that encroaches on its own data,' i.e., a question whose object is the questioner, a question we can't be detached from and objective about because we're always personally involved. Falling in love, e.g., is a mystery. Getting to Mars is a problem."[5] If humans were solvable problems, we'd be at a point of poetic paralysis since the engine driving all of our songs, stories, and poems is the mystery of what it means to be a person. Human nature is *always* personal—there is no view from nowhere. We can't shed our humanity to gain a better perspective on its limitations. We can't fully solve a problem that implicates us. While it's true that the various fields of therapy and psychology yield tremendous insights, there are no psychological and spiritual experts in the truest sense.[6]

Unwittingly, many parents fall into the trap of seeing their kids as problems. If we survey the cultural landscape, it's not hard to see why. Our world is awash with metrics. Measuring is second nature to modern people. But when we measure, we're doing more than simply crunching numbers. The multitude of measurements communicates ownership to us.

Recall a disconcerting episode in the life of King David: David summons Joab and the commanders of his army and orders a census of the nation of Israel. Joab is distressed by this order and begs the king to reconsider, but David overrules him. Swift punishment follows from the Lord, as the whole nation is engulfed with disease and pestilence (1 Chronicles 21:1-17). To our eyes this may look like a colossal overreaction on the part of God. The Lord is punishing David for playing God. Yes, he has installed David as Israel's king, but the nation remains his alone. In effect, David's census amounts to an act of irreverence and fatal pride. Joab's initial dismay was warranted. David's order was presuming ownership, and this pride unleashed God's judgment.

There's a sense in which our myriad tools of measurement offer us a kind of microcosm of David's pride. How often do you count your followers on social media, for instance? How closely do you monitor your children's lives? From personality tests to dating apps to social media to fitness software, we are in constant danger of being misled by our tools into thinking that we are our own.

But what happens when our tools fail? Pushed to their limits, many parents try to cope by outsourcing the problem to experts. That's when unwilling participants show up at youth events and Bible colleges get a grudging boost in their student population. Every year we see a flood of requests from brokenhearted moms and dads wanting a spiritual overhaul for their kids. What this would involve is left a bit vague, but the plan usually turns on getting the right information into the young person's brain: books, podcasts, conferences, one-on-one meetings, and regular video calls. Again, we're not opposed to any of these efforts so long as they're viewed as auxiliary. We take exception, however, when we're effectively asked to fill in for parents.

Sadly, the broken households scattered throughout our fallen world add a good deal of complexity to the situation. In many cases a single parent is forced to navigate all of this difficult territory on their own. With fostering and adoption we see yet another picture of the stark challenges facing so many families. Adding insult to injury is the feeling of judgment (both from oneself and others) that so often accompanies our efforts. The frequent glamorization of family life made possible by the highly selective vision of social media only exacerbates the problem. How often do we look through other people's posts and conclude that we simply don't measure up as moms and dads? But though our difficult circumstances inevitably play a role in shaping us, they need not define us. We labor side by side with our Lord and Savior, who offers to us his gentle yoke (Matthew 11:28-29). In a sense this is the most liberating part of the gospel invitation, namely, that our sins and brokenness don't need to define us. And to reiterate a point we made earlier: no matter what has happened, none of us are accidental parents. The Lord has entrusted us with this awesome blessing. Pastors, youth workers, apologists, and ministers of all stripes can lend a helping hand, but they cannot take our place as parents.

TAKING PROPER RESPONSIBILITY

We all need to remember that we belong to God—and those of us who are parents need to remember that our children belong to God. They are not problems awaiting solutions; they are gifts from our

Lord he has entrusted to us. And though we can't fix them, we are responsible for them. Naturally, we want to protect them from the onslaughts of this world, and we want to enlist all of the help we can get in this endeavor. But when our protectiveness degenerates into an ambition to control our kids, we've stumbled into the ubiquitous modern tendency to confuse mysteries with problems. The idea that human beings are nothing more than the sum of their parts is scientific naturalism, not Christianity. Our sons and daughters need parents, not technicians.

If you've fully grasped that your child is not a solvable problem, you'll quickly see that their salvation isn't in your hands. One of the most liberating aspects of mystery is that it frees us from the burden of having to save our kids.

The shape of our spiritual responsibility to our children turns on our own walk with Christ. The Christian life is more caught than taught. Furtive glimpses of his dad's morning devotions, the look of wincing astonishment on the face of a newly baptized infant, the unassuming glory of the bread and cup in a small Austrian church service held in the upstairs of a corporate office—these were the windows into the faith for young Cameron. Life's routine trials brought more glimpses: Though they were far from perfect, it wasn't lost on Cameron that forgiveness was second nature to his parents. They didn't hold grudges, and they didn't tear others down. Nor did they grieve "as those without hope" when death intruded on their lives. There was spiritual stability and resilience that life could not hammer out of them, and the source of this strength was clearly not part of our withering world. For his parents, Christianity was not some passing fashion or a convenient lifestyle; it was a way of life and it circumscribed every aspect of their existence.

True faithfulness is visible, and it's the mark of Christ's witnesses. This is part of what it means to "let your light shine before others, so that they may see your good works and give glory to your Father who is in heaven" (Matthew 5:16). Good parents are not experts, influencers, thought leaders, or apologists; they are faithful witnesses whose lives bring glory to God.

Writing to his young pastoral protégé, the apostle Paul offers a lovely tribute to the legacy of faith in Timothy's family:

> I am reminded of your sincere faith, a faith that dwelt first in your grandmother Lois and your mother Eunice and now, I am sure, dwells in you as well. For this reason I remind you to fan into flame the gift of God, which is in you through the laying on of my hands, for God gave us a spirit not of fear but of power and love and self-control. (2 Timothy 1:5-7)

Together, these devout women have instilled a lasting faith in Timothy, so much so that Paul can readily discern their lasting influence in Timothy's life. Here we have a beautiful picture of the redemptive ways our families can shape us. Conversely, we also see the tragedy endured by those who grew up outside the church. For Stuart the road to Christianity was long and treacherous, largely because neither of his parents followed Christ. With two parents deeply committed to the Lord, Cameron's experience was gloriously different. Though he endured his share of trials, Cameron's childhood was filled with the majesty of God's Word, the wonder of his sacraments, and the homely beauty of his church—all things that any child can accept and that nobody can outgrow.

But not all of us have a Timothy. Sadly, it's often the reverse, and we continue to plead for the spiritual well-being of our children as they wander far from the arms of Christ. Many of us find ourselves in the position of Monica, mother to Augustine of Hippo. Before he was revered as the great doctor of the church, Augustine was a spectacularly gifted scholar and a thoroughgoing hedonist, with no interest in Christianity. Not only did Monica continue to love him unconditionally, she steadfastly persisted in praying for her prodigal son. Monica's tears are a powerful rejoinder to our era of parental outsourcing. While she eagerly sought the counsel of brilliant spiritual voices who might reach her son, she never abdicated her parental responsibility by outsourcing Augustine's spiritual education. Though many faithful and gifted servants contributed to Augustine's eventual conversion—the teachings of Ambrose of Milan played an instrumental role in his thought—the picture of Monica's faithful life and persistent prayers for her son underscores the massive importance of a parent's spiritual influence. Indeed, so prominent is her role in Augustine's spiritual autobiography, *The Confessions*, that many theologians call her the unsung hero of the book.

With this in mind, we feel it's fitting to bring this chapter to a close with Augustine's heartfelt tribute to his parents. For Augustine both parent and child are ultimately children of God bound for their eternal home in the new Jerusalem. It's our prayer that these words will serve as both a challenge and an encouragement to you if you currently find yourself in Monica's position. May you know the Lord's strength as you seek to faithfully model Christ for your children, no matter where they are:

> From their flesh you brought me into this life, though how I do not know. Let them remember with loving devotion these two who were my parents in this transitory light, but also were my brethren under you, our Father, with our mother the Catholic Church, and my fellow-citizens in the eternal Jerusalem, for which your people sighs with longing throughout its pilgrimage, from its setting out to its return.[7]

Biographical Interlude

STUART'S STORY

Therefore if anyone is in Christ, he is a new creation.
The old has passed away; behold, the new has come.

2 Corinthians 5:17

At home my dad would often tell us a story about big and little wolves—a kind of crude Darwinian myth in which the big wolves always ruled the smaller wolves. The moral was clear: If you're a big wolf, you call the shots. If you're a little wolf, know your place and don't cross the big wolf. Clearly, the social Darwinism of the time was exercising a powerful if unacknowledged influence on our home life.

The fact that my mother took exception to this ruthless vision didn't stop us from internalizing it as a family. In *After Virtue*, Alasdair MacIntyre shows us why these kinds of stories are much more than family anecdotes:

> Through hearing stories about wicked stepmothers, lost children, good but misguided kings, wolves that suckle twin boys, youngest sons who receive no inheritance but must make their way in the world, and eldest sons who waste their inheritance on riotous living and go into exile to live with the swine, children learn or mislearn both what a child and what a parent is, what the cast of characters may be in the drama they have been born into and what the ways of the world are.[1]

For better or for worse my dad had introduced me to a meager cast in a savage drama, and though he didn't know it at the time, the consequences would soon be spelled out in my young adult life.

I was born in Glasgow, Scotland, in 1957. At that time Glasgow was an industrial city that had flourished largely because of its access to the sea and a labor force working in coal mining, steel production, and shipbuilding. I was born in the east end of the city, in Shettleston, which was a working-class district facing the challenges of the post–World War II era. In those years Britain was wrestling with its national identity in the face of its imperial decline and ongoing austerity measures imposed by the war years.

I grew up in a home that was shaped by my mother's defection from the faith of her childhood, which she viewed as narrow and repressive, as well as my dad's experiences as a WWII veteran from a broken household with radical leftist leanings. He had dreams of the new possibilities opened up by the promises of a welfare state and was excited to build a new life with his bride.

My early childhood memories were quite happy. I had many friends and lots of time and space to play and have adventures. This was a time well before the smartphone hegemony, and we would roam far and wide until the end of each day. Things at home were not so easy. Though socially outgoing, I was a moody and impetuous child prone to registering my displeasure with loud fits and temper tantrums. Consequently, I often found myself on the wrong side of my parents and my father in particular. Indeed, his low estimation of me seemed to be growing more pronounced every day.

From an early age I hated bullies, and once I was in school I found myself defending the "smaller wolves" with my fists. On one occasion the class bully was picking on a younger boy. I intervened and told the bully to leave him alone. He then tried to fight me, which turned into a real scrap, but I got the upper hand. To my surprise the boy I'd rescued wasn't grateful for my intervention; he simply feared me now instead of the bully. It seems I was now the big wolf.

As I was excelling in the world of physical combat, my dad was doing well in his job as a sales executive in a large retail business, and our lifestyle soon reflected his professional success. Concerned with the increasing gang violence in our neighborhood, my parents bought a house in a more affluent district on the outskirts of Glasgow called Milngavie (pronounced Mulguy: don't ask), and we made the move when I was thirteen. I hated it from day one.

This was the early 1970s, and I was just awakening to music and the world of teenage rebellion. I soaked up music from bands like T-Rex, David Bowie, and The Who—whose infamous "My Generation" remains an anthem for disaffected youth. I quickly made new friends and found those who also hated school, wrestled with authority, and wanted to party. The world around us was changing, and we felt it. The world seemed on the verge of some kind of major cataclysm. There was less respect for authority and many inducements to pursue our own pleasures and freedom. The shadow of the cold war hung over us, and nuclear apocalypse was always a threat.

According to MacIntyre, "There is no way to give us an understanding of any society, including our own, except through the stock of stories which constitute its initial dramatic resources."[2] Movies were my key dramatic resources. I reveled in stories of WWII and loved films like *The Great Escape*, *633 Squadron*, and *The Guns of Navarone*. In a major departure from my dad's Darwinian script, I developed a love for the struggle between good and evil and these heroic characters who faced danger and took on the bad guys. It all added to my dream to somehow be like that! They fed into my emerging vision of good and evil and some kind of moral framework of the universe. Around the mid-1970s, however, I was drawn to a very different kind of movie. In watching Clint Eastwood in *Dirty Harry* and Charles Bronson in *Death Wish* the vision of vigilante justice first gripped me. These tough, fearless loners who took on evil, bucked the system, and fought for justice were compelling to me. In contrast to the lone wolf, maybe it was the image of the hero that began to attract me. They stood apart and stood up for what they felt was right—outlaw and hero. They were not accepted in the normal places of life but were clearly opposed to the criminals and became agents of justice. So, in some ways they stood out from the crowd, ready to defend or act where needed. But in the vigilante hero, I encountered a figure that wed my poor man's Darwinism to my sense of justice. On some level, in some way, I wanted to be like them. I wanted to do what they did. I think that some of my fights at school, some of the situations I jumped into, were fueled by this subconscious motivation. This is what cultural catechesis looks like on the ground.

Part of life in Scotland for young people, then as well as now, is the pull of drinking at an early age. I began drinking with my friends when I was thirteen years old and soon became adept at procuring alcohol whenever we wanted it. The trick was to keep the wool pulled over my parents' eyes. Though I had blown it on several occasions, one incident in particular marked a turning point in my life. A friend and I ditched school to get drunk, but we decided to make an appearance as class was in session. Both of us were belligerent and disruptive, and I ended up brandishing a knife. Fortunately, no one was physically hurt, but this foolish outburst marked the official end of my high school career. I was summoned on the following day with my dad to see the headmaster, and he was willing to let me stay under strict conditions. When I made it clear that I was not interested, leaving became the only option. Understandably, my parents were at their wits' end, but all I could think of was how to escape from their oppressive clutches and my deep unhappiness. I had tried running away once already but got caught and was deeply frustrated.

It all came to a head a few weeks later when I came home one night from drinking with my friends and smelled strongly of alcohol. My dad flew into a rage and we ended up in a fistfight. My seething anger caught him by surprise. I was also quite big at this point and no stranger to fights. I am saddened when I think back on this time, but I see it as a culmination of built-up resentment, nonexistent communication, and deep anger. Dad and I were constantly at odds, which was exhausting. We argued incessantly, and when he drank things got even worse. Dad was used to giving commands, lecturing, or making threats, but he was unprepared for any serious resistance. I increasingly rejected it all and doubted anything he had to say. I just wanted to get away and be free. Thanks to this vicious fight, I got my wish—a few days later I moved into a cheap flat in the west end of the city. Hard to believe: I was fifteen and on my own. Much to his chagrin, my dad discovered that I had internalized his little Darwinist script. He had raised a big wolf.

Several influences were shaping me at this time. First was the music of Alice Cooper. His voice, the Grand Guignol style, the brooding chaos—it all gripped me. I also was introduced to the world of kung fu movies and a new star—Bruce Lee! I had never seen anything like him. This small powerhouse of a man who subdued all his opponents when he was consistently outnumbered, outgunned, and outsized was an inspiration! I wanted this. I enrolled in karate classes and took it all very seriously. My flatmate shared similar passions, and we decorated all the walls of our flat with posters and huge images from *Enter the Dragon*, *Fist of Fury*, and many others. This was our iconography. I woke up to Lee's fighting stances or combat scenes as a daily feature of my world. It all contributed to my ideal of the archetypal tough guy.

I worked for a couple of years in menswear stores as a sales-person. I did quite well at this and as a result was recruited for a new store owned by a male model and popular TV star in Scotland. For a season I entered the world of men's fashion and may have stayed in that space permanently except for a chance meeting one afternoon in the new store opened by my bosses in Sauchiehall Street, one of Glasgow's main shopping centers. One afternoon a customer asked if I was interested in being a bouncer. I asked what was involved and what it paid. He told me that he managed a large disco that was next door to our shop and that they needed security guards to patrol the dance floors, protect the doors, and help stop fights or troublemakers. It would bring extra cash, and of course there were lots of girls as an added incentive.

I took the job, complete with the compulsory white shirt, bow tie, and dinner jacket as the uniform to make us stand out. The task was clear. Look out for troublemakers, stop any fights, and be on the lookout for weapons or gang activities. We were to be ready to jump into any situation and subdue those who were causing trouble and expel them. I now found myself in a world that somewhat matched my fantasies about rugged heroes and vigilante justice. The disco itself was a large venue with two main dance floors and multiple bars. It was open on the weekends and drew a large, young crowd. I loved it from day one.

I also made friends quickly and was amazed by a man I met by the name of Robbie. I had never seen anyone like him. He was not tall but easily one of the broadest men I had ever seen, with huge muscles bulging from his jacket. He came from the south side of Glasgow, an area notorious for its thug culture and ensuing gang violence. We were in the changing room one night, and I was in my jeans and T-shirt. Robbie came over, pulled on my shirt, and said to me with disdain, "Nice shirt. How come you didn't buy one with muscles in it?" Naturally, my embarrassment was only intensified by the fact that this jab at my stature was coming from a mini–Arnold Schwarzenegger! Just to be clear, this man had a chest as deep as a barrel and arms and muscles like nothing I had ever seen. By contrast I had no muscles, no physique to speak of. In the world of the disco, looking like an amateur wrestler gave you cachet and respect. It set me thinking. I also met at that time another Stuart, a man much bigger and wilder than me. We became instant friends. It wasn't long before we garnered a reputation and earned the nickname "the two Stuarts."

Meanwhile, Robbie took a break from his insults and invited me to the gym, where he trained in weightlifting and powerlifting. It was a slow start, but I was consistent and eventually excelled in this arena. I was looking more and more like a big wolf or the big thug, depending on how you look at it: I put on weight, lifted larger loads, and felt more and more aggressive as I got bigger and stronger. Going to the gym, being with these tough men, training hard, and seeing the results of this hard work in my body and my look increased my self-assurance and strengthened my resolve to be a man as ruthless as he was relentless.

In a maneuver not unlike *Taxi Driver*'s Travis Bickle, I remember one night planning for a way to meet some thugs and surprise them with my version of swift justice. I was at that time driving a very high-end Toyota, which was aqua blue and metallic. It was a big luxury vehicle and stood out in any setting. I drove to a particularly rough spot in a district called Maryhill. With two shotguns in my trunk, I parked half on the sidewalk and sat on the hood of the car and waited. I felt sure the car would attract attention and that sitting there might draw some angry young men to pick a fight. I was dressed in my leather jacket and inwardly daring some lowlife to try and steal my car.

Even though I knew many others who had received honest muggings on this same street, nothing happened to me. I sat there brooding. I watched. I waited. I glared, all to no end. My plans to show off my vigilante skills were thwarted by the confounding indifference of this shady spot. Looking back, this whole episode is equal parts horrifying and pathetic. What would've happened if someone *had* approached me? Sadly, we're in a cultural moment where we see the catastrophic results of crossing juvenile fantasies with real violence on a near-daily basis. In this case the Lord in his mercy spared me from shedding any blood. Eventually, I retreated to my flat for an infuriatingly quiet night bereft of any vigilante antics.

Occasionally, I would visit my parents and flaunt these new developments in my life. Despite his earlier stories about big and small wolves, my dad disapproved of my appearance as I had bulked up, consumed huge amounts of food and supplements, and courted the look of a hard man. It was all a performance in many respects, but I can only imagine what my parents were thinking or feeling during this time.

I'm tempted to speculate that my dad may have seen some of his handiwork in my appearance. Years later I would be utterly captivated by Tim Burton's spin on *Batman*. Yes, I know that Christopher Nolan's films have relegated Burton's 1989 version to the dustbin, but I'm still impressed by its psychological depth. One scene in particular depicts a remarkable exchange between Batman and the Joker. The Joker, played with gleeful abandon by Jack Nicholson, argues, "You made me. Remember? You dropped me into that vat of chemicals!" Batman responds, "You killed my parents. . . . You made me first."[3] These lines always haunted me. In many ways it's the kind of existential response I could have leveled at my dad during those years. He may have disapproved of my particular path, but I had followed his script to the letter.

I now saw the world in simple terms. I lived for myself, my wants, and my needs. Nothing else mattered. I said goodbye to the sedate world of menswear. As a result of my connections in the dance hall, I met one of the better-known heavies in the Glasgow underworld. We'll call him Morris. He owned a car business and had club connections in the city. He needed drivers to help pick up used cars for resale and to do odd jobs for him, and I took up his offer. He liked me from the start, and over time I took on more and more tasks from him. He then asked me to manage one of his car show rooms, which I did. This meant more money, driving any car I chose, and connections with the kind of people I felt were significant. It was a world of big wolves. These were not people interested in anything much but their own pleasure, prosperity, and success. If they had a philosophy, it was survival of the smartest, toughest, or wiliest! It's important to stress that I never knew at that time how aligned my thinking was with crude expressions of social Darwinism. Survival of the fittest or the most aggressive, rampant hedonism, the law of the jungle—these were simply our tacit assumptions. We weren't reading or writing books on the subject; we were simply living it.

At this time I was asked by an old friend to help a woman he knew, called Clare, to recover her stuff from her ex-boyfriend. Despite her many attempts to get it back, he had steadfastly refused. The two Stuarts were promptly summoned and the ex-boyfriend was quickly persuaded to return his former girlfriend's possessions. Shortly after her rescue, we began a relationship. Things were looking good for me. I had my own place, drove nice cars, earned good money, and had an attractive live-in girlfriend. What more could I ask for? Little did I know that I just reached another crucial turning point in my life.

One day Clare asked me what I thought of Jesus. The short answer was nothing. I had seldom given it any thought and believed Christianity didn't even rise to the dignity of critique; it was simply an irrelevance. I had no interest in or any desire for God, the gods, or anything of that nature. The conversation did not go far, and I assumed it was just a passing fancy. How wrong I was. My girlfriend was on a spiritual quest. She was hungry for answers and needed to know if God existed and if Christianity had something to say. Unbeknownst to me, she had been talking to a Christian colleague at work and then finally in desperation went into a church and asked the pastor how she could come to know God. He happily obliged, and she gave her life to Christ. It was a real encounter, one she could not deny and was eager to share.

When she told me of this encounter, I was dumbfounded. At first I thought, *so what?* As long as it did not change anything in my life, in our lives, then whatever! But the transformation in her was real, and it became clear that we had to separate. I was angry and confused. What was this? Who were these people who had messed with her thinking and our life? I knew nothing about religion and almost nothing about Christianity. Like so many modern people outside of the church, I assumed it was something people chose as a lifestyle preference and nothing more. From what I could see, the church seemed to be a haven for people who were too scared to face reality. Whatever it was, it was certainly not the place for me!

After a couple of weeks apart, Clare called and invited me to meet the colleague and the colleague's husband who had influenced her. Though it pains me to say it, I went to their home firmly resolved to physically assault them. But I was surprised by the serenity of their home and by their manner and comportment. An ineffable quality permeated the atmosphere in this home. Something was different.

Nevertheless, I sought to undermine all that was shared by them. I contested the idea of a God and the relevance of any of it for our daily lives. Slowly, steadily, and surely they shared Scripture, answered questions, covered objections, and laid out the gospel. There were no clever methodologies, slick gimmicks, or cutting-edge techniques. Simply two faithful witnesses sharing the treasure of Christ's gospel in earthen vessels (2 Corinthians 4:7). In a word, Christ's sheep shared his words of life with the big wolf. And, as the apostle Paul says so well, the Lord's strength is made perfect in our weakness (2 Corinthians 12:8-10). I entered their home an unbeliever, and while there I began to have a creeping sense that there may be some truth in it all—and then began to fear it was true! There was a God, and I needed a savior.

I went upstairs to their bathroom and knelt and prayed. I asked God to save me and to forgive my sins and all the damage I had done thus far. When I came down the stairs and shared, they all hugged me and prayed with me. A new life had begun. The wolf had become one of Christ's sheep. I had no idea what had happened and the impact it would all have. The young couple who led me to the Lord subsequently opened their home to me and introduced me to the church. I began to attend this small congregation and was encouraged to read the Bible daily and to pray. I was given the basic orientation for an ongoing walk with Christ, which had to include Scripture, prayer, and good fellowship. The foundations were being laid.

It's impossible to overstate the significance of this lovely couple opening their hearts and home to me. I was a spiritual infant, woefully unprepared to face the manifold challenges of abandoning my former life alone. I shared countless meals with these people, said many prayers with them, and searched the Scriptures with their guidance. We quickly identified a destructive pattern that unfolded on Saturday nights and often kept me from church. Sunday was a very special time for me, and our worship service centered on prayer and the Lord's Supper, which was profoundly moving for me. But old habits were hard to shake, and my former life kept beckoning in the form of bouts of aggression and ensuing brawls. Seeing this, my friends invited me to stay at their home on

Saturday nights. I could come when I wanted, as late as needed, and it gave me a sanctuary, a place where I could be quiet and prepare for worship. They were my spiritual parents and made it clear they were there for me, and they demonstrated this by their constant availability to me.

It wasn't long before my newfound faith met with serious consequences as I shared it in my workplace and as I tried to work out my complicated relationship with Clare and my own past. I quickly came to see the hostility to the gospel and the cost of commitment as each day passed. My old friends thought I had lost my mind and worked tirelessly to deconvert me in the early stages, even going so far as to plaster the walls of my office with hard-core pornography. I was discovering firsthand what it meant to embody what Martin Luther called "the way of the cross"—a manner of life that looks like lunacy to those who haven't bowed the knee to Christ. For my part I wanted to deepen my understanding of the faith and was hungry to grow and to serve. A few weeks after my conversion I attended a summer camp where I heard some deep teaching about the needs on the mission field. I was convinced that I needed to follow and serve Christ more fully, and I felt called to go, no matter where he sent. Soon, I was recruited by Operation Mobilization (OM) to work with a team serving the communist countries in Eastern and Central Europe. Our base of operations was in Vienna, Austria.

A stark reversal was taking place in my life. Whereas before I had been captivated by the enticements of hedonism and vigilante justice, now I was called to forsake everything, take up my cross, and follow Christ. I sold possessions, paid for outfitting a coffee bar in my church, bought some household appliances for my mother, donated the rest of my savings to missions, and left home—and all that was familiar—for an unknown world and life. From now on I would trust in the Lord's provision rather than in my own strength and ingenuity. If I had wanted wealth and power before, all I wanted now was to serve Christ.

My years in Vienna would play a central role in my Christian formation. For one thing, I met the woman who would become my wife in this beautiful city. Mary was an American, and like me she was a convert and had a deep passion for the gospel and mission. Our romance bloomed amid the welter of vigorous travel, Bible smuggling, and brief stints in prison for distributing "Christian propaganda" in communist nations. We were eventually married in the United States. Both of us tried to envision what a Christian home would look like, but it was difficult to imagine in the context of this strange life we were jointly called to.

Soon the speculation would end. Our son, Cameron, was born in 1984 and our daughter, Katherine, followed in 1986. Though we were thrilled with the gift of two kids, the circumstances of our missionary life remained challenging. This was still before the advent of smartphones, and I traveled extensively. To make matters worse, my trips were often to parts of the world where communication was limited or nonexistent. I was often off the grid. Mary carried a huge load not only because we were far from both of our respective families but also because she was managing the daily chaos of two small children in a foreign country. Fortunately, she had several close friends who were also navigating the struggles of being young mothers. There were also older women with kids a bit more mature who could offer advice and support in managing the ups and downs of family life in a strange land.

Like so many young Christian families, we read books, observed others, and talked incessantly about how to raise our kids. Mary did a great job of making our family meals a time and place for good food and rich conversations. At her insistence we shared all of our meals, and the kitchen table became a key symbol of the communal ethos of our household. Because she spent more time with the kids than I did, she was able to see subtleties that I missed. We discussed attitudes and behaviors and tried to aim for ways to keep the discipline to a minimum. Our primary aim was to cultivate discernment and well-ordered love—not to gain total control. We wanted to cultivate genuine hunger for Christ in our kids. I had a brooding concern that being born in a Christian home might somehow inoculate them against the faith. Would our inconsistencies undermine our testimony and send mixed signals about our life in Christ to these young souls? I still ask myself this question.

Why was this anxiety about hypocrisy such a dominant concern for me? I was aware that my upbringing had given me a jaded picture of parenting, and I was deeply conscious of the person I had been before I met the Lord. As Pascal exhorts us, "Men despise religion. They hate it and are afraid it may be true. The cure for this is first to show that religion is not contrary to reason, but worthy of reverence and respect. *Next make it attractive, make good men wish it were true, and then show that it is.*"[4] But even with the best of intentions I knew that I was still human—that I was selfish and could not live consistently all the time. I feared that my kids would see this frailty, interpret it as hypocrisy, and reject the faith because we didn't make it attractive. We determined as a couple that perfection was not an option (nor a possibility), but honesty and humility would be. We would model the broken authority that characterizes those who have taken up their cross.

In the late 1990s Mary and I sensed a change coming in our lives and were delighted by an offer to join Ravi Zacharias's team in Atlanta. We had never imagined living in the United States, and though Mary was born there she had lived for many years outside of the country, so in many respects it was a new place for her as well. We were all caught up initially in the excitement of the move, of a new country, new experiences, and so many new opportunities.

We bought our first home in the Greater Atlanta area and settled into a new kind of ministry: apologetics. The kids made friends but began to show some signs of struggle. They were growing, entering the teen years, and facing the usual challenges of figuring out who they were and what they wanted. Katherine struggled with the strongly expressed sense of American exceptionalism so dominant in the South. Cameron was attracted to the cultural fringes, carving out space within the black metal subculture.

During these first years in the United States, both kids had issues. Katherine began skipping school, and we saw a brooding resentment against all authority increasingly characterizing her behavior. Cameron continued his voyage into the nihilistic seas of black metal. We talked and continued to try to encourage them to be active in church, to meet other Christian friends, but they both had their share of stories of "Christian" kids having sex, getting drunk, and keeping up appearances while living the party life. They were not persuaded by or attracted to what they saw.

This was the very thing I dreaded. We were facing a form of nominal Christianity that simply wasn't an option in the predominantly secular world of Europe. Here, many kids were adept at performing for their parents and pastors. In effect, they were functional atheists: they professed Christ but lived as though he didn't exist.

Authenticity was a vital concern for us. I did not want my kids to perform the American cultural spin on the gospel. At the same time I was also concerned that they would fool themselves into thinking that God turned a blind eye to their lack of commitment. Though we were careful to allow them room to work through these issues on their own, we steadfastly refused to allow them to hide from their inconsistencies. Mary and I were determined to press the kids to seriously wrestle with God. We wanted them to have a living faith. If it was real, it would bear fruit. We knew that only God could conquer the heart, but we also knew that our primary responsibility as their parents was to be faithful witnesses, even when that meant challenging their moral lethargy and spiritual apathy.

I felt a particular burden for my kids because I had not felt approval or much acceptance from my dad. Cameron struggled with how he perceived I felt about him. It was a classic Catch-22. I wanted to show acceptance, approval, and love, but I also wanted to see change and to see him (and Katherine) flourish!

After several encounters in which I attempted to raise the questions of character and of consistent living in light of a faith profession, our communication became seriously strained. Mary and I were praying, and we were worried. We knew of destructive influences in Cameron's life that would carry a cost. Cameron was increasingly withdrawn, agitated, and spiritually apathetic. One morning, after much thinking and prayer on my part, Cameron sauntered into the kitchen. He grunted some casual greeting, and I asked a question: "Son, why do you call yourself a Christian?" My hope was once again to cause some reflection on what being a Christian really meant.

As it turns out this simple question would play a pivotal role in Cameron's spiritual recovery. At the time, however, he was less than thrilled with this early morning invitation for a moral inventory of his spiritual life: "It's six in the morning, Dad," he said. "Do you think we could talk about this later?"

As you can imagine, this was not the response I'd hoped for. "Oh, that's just perfect, isn't it?" I blurted out and headed for my library in the basement. The conversation may have ended abruptly, but my question was just the beginning. I'll let Cameron tell you the rest in his story.

PART TWO

A FATHER'S RESPONSE TO THE THREE MISCONCEPTIONS

4

CULTIVATING DISCERNMENT

Solid food is for the mature, who because of practice
have their senses trained to discern good and evil.

HEBREWS 5:14 NASB

I n a brief conversation with a young father one day about this book, he raised a common concern found in many Christian homes today. Talking with other parents in his circles, he pointed to the deep-seated desire to uncover some fail-safe parental technique or method that would guarantee a dazzling array of trophies, dean's lists, mission trips, and upwardly mobile careers. In short, he was looking for a guarantee of success. When life's routine calamities interrupt these dreams, however, the result is often anger and confusion—a sense of betrayal. Did God not promise that if we followed the steps, kept the rules, and used the instruction manuals that the outcome would be guaranteed? Why then do our kids continue to struggle with their faith? Why do they fail to apply the lessons imparted to them in our homes?

The unvoiced assumption seems to be that the exhortations of Scripture to "train up a child in the way he should go" function like some kind of spiritual software that ushers in automatic transformation. This is a simple but profound misunderstanding of the biblical picture of wisdom. As we've seen, our modern world tends to foster the three broad misconceptions in some Christian parents:

fear protects, information saves, and spiritual education belongs to experts. Consequently, we regard the surrounding culture with deep suspicion, scan the Scriptures for saving information, and, if we encounter something that eludes our grasp, we seek professionals who can solve the problem for us. Experts rule!

But the biblical understanding of wisdom has to do with more than knowledge. It has to do with skilled living. Presently, we have access to reams and reams of information. Most of us are overwhelmed by the daily deluge of it on our phones. We have no shortage of information and knowledge, but the social fabric of our culture continues to fray. Depression, anxiety, and suicide levels are surging, and mental-health professionals are struggling to address the epidemic. When it comes to information, we've got an embarrassment of riches. Yet we still don't know how to live. If you want a poignant example of the limitations of mere information, look no further than the state of our nation.

To live well is a perennial challenge, and the most common source of this difficulty is not a lack of information, but a conflict of loves. With this in mind, I remember an incident that occurred between my older brother and me when we were boys. Model building was a great passion of mine at the time, and my side of our room was filled with the fruits of my labors. Small planes, tanks, and ships lined my shelves, and I was always eager to add new additions to my small fleet. On this particular occasion, I had nearly completed an elaborate version of the luxury ship *Queen Elizabeth II*. It sat in the room awaiting the final details of paint and decals. During an argument with my brother, unable to get my way (my good), I got so angry with him, I took his cricket bat and smashed my model into a hundred pieces. At first glance this may look like nothing more than a juvenile outburst. On closer inspection, however, it gives us insight into the complexity of living well.

To clarify this complexity let's place my competing loves in this story on a gradient scale. On the one hand we've got my love of model building. More than a wholesome hobby, the full realization of this pursuit was independent of my own will in the sense that I had to follow the rules to see the project completed successfully. I had to submit to the vision and values of the manufacturer. I was free to deviate from the instructions, of course, but my model would suffer the consequences. Ideally, my will would be in alignment with the microcosmic world of the model. If I wanted to succeed, I had to submit to the rules of its instructions. In this sense, model building required me to move "with the grain of the universe."[1]

On the other hand we have my selfish love that prioritizes my own will over everything else. Unlike my love of model building, success in this department does not operate independently of my will. Indeed, as this story shows, the successful appeasement of one's will often comes at one's own expense. In this case my selfish love for having my way at any cost outweighed my love of model building, and I satisfied my desire by destroying something else that I loved.

Sadly, this conflict was not limited to model ships, and as I grew older I destroyed items of much greater significance. How many of us have stood in the wreckage of broken relationships and honestly wrestled with the fact that, to a significant degree, we've gotten what we wanted? How many of us can look at the damage in our lives and see the incriminating marks of our selfish desires? Think of the psychological acuity of Paul's remarks in Romans 7:15: "I do not understand my own actions. For I do not do what I want, but I do the very thing I hate." We can know our basic conundrum inside out, but that's not enough to stop us from smashing the things we love on a routine basis. We need more than knowledge. We need wisdom and the power to live life the way it was intended.

My own home life had shaped in me a largely unconscious view of life as a struggle. If survival constituted our most noble aspiration, it paid to be ruthless and aggressive. Be the *big wolf*. At least, that's what my dad would have me believe. For all its inherent ruthlessness, this worldview was remarkably simple from a moral standpoint. Use your power (and your wits) to get what you want. This basic philosophy had led me to drop out of school and leave home at age fifteen. It then took me to a successful career as a criminal in Glasgow's underworld. What I failed to take into account was my consistent propensity for smashing things I loved. Just as my powers had led me to demolish my beloved *Queen Elizabeth II*, so my present desires were frequently inflicting damage on my own life and those around me.

Reading the Bible and meeting real Christians opened up a new world for me by complicating my moral vision. My moral life and my decisions could not be anchored merely in my subjective preferences and feelings; they needed to conform to reality. I came to see that there was an objective, independent moral structure to life, one that demanded my surrender. I needed to not only be challenged but to be changed.

Things grew even more complicated when I joined OM and began smuggling Bibles and Christian literature into communist nations in the late 1970s. In this context the simple sentiments and easy black-and-white judgments of well-meaning Christians in their suburban homes in the affluent West rang hollow amid the panoply of daily deceptions in an irrational, totalitarian regime. Honing in on this strained social dynamic, Czeslaw Milosz points to the need for citizens (and especially state officials) to become expert actors.

Such acting is a highly developed craft that places a premium upon mental alertness. Before it leaves the lips, every word must be evaluated as to its consequences. A smile that appears at the wrong moment, a glance that is not all it should be can occasion dangerous suspicions and accusations. Even one's gestures, tone of voice, or preference for certain kinds of neckties are interpreted as signs of one's political tendencies.[2]

The believers behind the Iron Curtain didn't even have the luxury of a carefree trip to the grocery store to get the items they wanted. Something as simple as buying coffee required careful prayer and discernment since it was an item that was frequently only available on the black market. Given Milosz's strained description, such luxury items might also signify Western "decadence" to state officials.

Moral reasoning, I discovered, was complex. My own experience crossing borders with Bibles and Christian books in concealed compartments in our vehicles, facing corrupt police in Eastern European countries and using various forms of dishonesty (hidden compartments, aliases, concealed addresses, etc.) to protect those we were trying to serve alerted me to the need for a more robust discernment and moral imagination. Many situations didn't come with ready-made answers or simple solutions that could be quickly and painlessly applied. The need, I soon understood, was to learn to cultivate wisdom, discernment, and courage, and this would remain a constant challenge for me.

COUNTERING FEAR WITH DISCERNMENT

Wisdom is a neglected topic in a culture that prioritizes technique and methodology. But the idea of a way to live in consistent recognition of God's presence, under his authority, and for his glory (*coram Deo*) is vital. The wisdom tradition is designed to help shape skills in living—giving attention to God's words, being diligent to not let them depart from one's mind, and keeping them in one's heart. Why? Because they are *life* to those who find them and *health* to the whole body. At the center of all of this is the well-known Scripture that warns us to "keep [our] heart with all vigilance" because "from it flow the springs of life" (Proverbs 4:23).

Though training and education play an indispensable part, discernment is learned in the practical details and outworking of everyday life. Recognizing the moral complexity of my competing desires was one thing, but navigating the spiritual wasteland of the Soviet Union and the Eastern Bloc opened my eyes to a whole new level of life's difficulty. My journey of faith also allowed me to observe many expressions of the Christian faith, not only different denominations but also the different ways it's lived in many different countries. I observed rich treasures and practices in various homes. Deep hospitality and incredible generosity in a Baptist home in Poland. Serious prayer and devotion in a Lutheran home in Germany. Abounding joy and passionate expectation of God's blessing in a Pentecostal home in Peru. God's gift of creativity and skills in an Anglican home in India, and I could add more. Each brought something unique, some aspect of God's truth and work, and over time I learned that I had to cultivate eyes to see the rich tapestry of God's abundance on display throughout the globe. God was at work in ways that I could scarcely imagine!

Reflecting on Proverbs 4:23, the value of a transformed heart is surely where the Bible leads us. The instruction aims to shape us into the kind of people who can handle any of life's challenges, whether they involve abundance or scarcity. This aim is evident in Paul's words to the Philippians: "I know how to be brought low, and I know how to abound. In any and every circumstance, I have learned the secret of facing plenty and hunger, abundance and need" (Philippians 4:12). Don't miss Paul's holistic emphasis here: In a fallen world our "successes" are just as liable to ruin our souls as any form of failure. Think of my former life in the Glasgow underworld. There was no shortage of money, power, and pleasure at my disposal. Yet my success there was nearly my undoing.

Years later, I would experience a dramatic reversal in a prison cell in Eastern Europe. My teammates and I had been apprehended at the border on one of our Bible distribution missions. In short order our heads were shaved, our passports were confiscated, and we found ourselves effectively stripped of all our rights. As terrifying as the situation was, I can honestly say that each of us experienced true joy in that squalid cell. Though each of our personal Bibles was impounded, the Holy Spirit brought a flood of verses to our minds, and we spoke them all out loud. We also sang hymns and thanked the Lord for every bite of prison slop that was delivered to us on our filthy meal trays. This is a picture of what it means to face scarcity with eager expectation and joy. Paul is celebrating the spiritual liberty of being able to endure both need and abundance. In our context here in the West, I think we struggle most with the latter.

But the wisdom of bringing my entire personality under the authority of Christ remained a challenge. I remember being stunned one day as I listened to a visiting friend, David, who was a management consultant. He had been tasked with helping our team in Vienna to work together more effectively. During one of his teaching sessions, he said, "We do what we value, not what we believe." I was taken aback and immediately protested. After all, we were missionaries deeply convinced of the truth and the priority of God's Word. We had uprooted our families to live in a foreign nation and devote our lives to its people. How were we not putting what we believed into practice? Our imaginations were constantly being challenged by stories of pioneers who laid down their lives for Christ in difficult places and circumstances. We were also inspired by those who forsook all and went to unreached peoples or translated the Bible or trusted God to do the impossible and reach the most resistant groups or nations. There was an expectancy that God was active by his Spirit all the time and an urgency that we needed to be attentive to his will and his way. At this point I had been walking with Christ for a good number of years, and I assumed the lessons had sunk in and were deeply owned. Yet as David spoke to us, I soon realized I still had much to learn.

With alarming simplicity David pointed out that though we all extolled the virtues of being servants, one of the major sources of conflict among us was the mounting pile of unwashed dishes in the kitchen sink. He also added the usual suspects of gossip and character assassination to the list. The more I thought about it, the more I saw how easy it was to conceal the actual truth of our motives and circumstances. True, we could all hide behind the camouflage of our Christian lingo, but the actual conditions of our office belied a very different set of convictions. This deep-seated penchant for self-deception drew me to the work of the writer M. Scott Peck. In his book *The People of the Lie*, Peck provides case after case of the creative strategies we use to hide from ourselves when confronted by facts that contradict our perceptions.[3] It might be something as simple as the unwashed dishes in the sink.

Peck brought me back to my small *Queen Elizabeth II* once again. While it was all too easy for me to verbally proclaim my devotion to Christ, this devotion was frequently undermined by the lure of the same selfish love that inspired me to wreck my little vessel with my brother's cricket bat. For all my spiritual growth since my conversion, I still struggled with the crucial distinction between my own will and that of my Lord. I was still a child, at times, throwing a temper tantrum. I also did not fully grasp the distinction between what I thought was my good and Christ's superior plan for my life—that these were not always in sync. Indeed, more often than not, they clashed. It was all too easy to embrace a form of simple moralism, where rights and wrongs were easily spelled out and where outward conformity could give the appearance of living in truth. (This issue is particularly pronounced in the North American church.)

The team dynamics in my office were a challenge, but what about my family? As young parents, Mary and I devoted a good deal of our prayers and thinking to showing our children what a life set apart for Christ looks like. We were especially focused on teaching them the distinction between outward appearances and inward realities. Mere conformity was not the goal. We wanted to make it clear to them that the Lord desired their hearts.

In our search as parents for ways to connect our spiritual convictions to everyday living, we found that certain movies and selected TV programs opened up space for discussions on competing worldviews and ideas that often conflicted with or outright denied Scripture. Rather than viewing these competing visions as a threat, however, Mary and I saw them as opportunities to explore the implications of our faith. Cameron calls this practice of unveiling the spiritual realities behind our various entertainments "apocalyptic realism." We didn't simply want our kids to consult with sources that cataloged expletives, sex scenes, and onscreen violence. We wanted them to learn to discern between good and evil. In *Areopagitica*, his celebrated tract against censorship, the poet John Milton argues,

> Since therefore the knowledge and survey of vice in this world is necessary to the constituting of human virtue, and the scanning of error to the confirmation of truth, how can we more safely, and with less danger, scout into the regions of sin and falsity than by reading all manner of tractates and hearing all manner of reason? And this is the benefit which may be had of books promiscuously read.[4]

No doubt, this quote might set off alarm bells for some readers, and Milton's wording is certainly provocative. But note the careful distinction he's making. He's arguing that the "survey of vice" and the "scanning of error" is necessary in "this world." That is, to cultivate a robust moral sensibility in a fallen world, it's crucial to gain a deeper understanding of the surrounding darkness.

Milton is no idealist, and he knows that true virtue can't make an appearance amid ignorance. It's in this sense that Milton distinguishes between "innocence" and "virtue."[5] In Milton's formulation, innocence is closer to ignorance while virtue constitutes a principled resistance to sin. If someone abstains from illegal drugs because they're blissfully unaware of the horrors of addiction, we can count it as fortunate, but it wouldn't be accurate to call it virtuous. Conversely, if someone makes a conscious decision to forgo the momentary gratification of illicit substances in favor of long-term well-being, we can rightly call that virtue.

When Milton asks, "How can we more safely, and with less danger, scout into the regions of sin and falsity than by reading all manner of tractates and hearing all manner of reason?" he makes it clear that he's not offering a carte blanche with regard to our cultural diet. He's calling for a safe approach that treads cautiously in the fallen terrain of our world. Mary and I wanted to avoid two tendencies we encountered with great frequency in our cloistered missionary community, namely, a fear-based approach that demonized "secular culture" and a naive insularity that mistook ignorance for virtue.

One particular "region of sin" that constitutes an intimate part of most of our lives is our entertainment. Movies and TV programs offer us the chance to help our kids navigate a cultural landscape that often stands in stark opposition to Christ's authority. The movie or program in question has been written and produced with specific intent. The layout of the scene, the lighting, the music, the nature of the dialogue, what was included and excluded from the camera—all of these elements are carefully planned. What does it say? What does it leave out? Why does the producer do it that particular way?

These kinds of discussions helped our kids to peer behind the curtain of many cultural assumptions and played an instrumental role in cultivating the skills of discernment. It's important to point out that neither Mary nor I simply approached these movies and shows with philosophical scalpels; we *enjoyed* them as well. I could point to the casual nihilism on display in most of our sitcoms without coming across as a legalistic killjoy. After all, I was laughing with everyone else. At the same time, enjoyment need not preclude careful reflection, and I aimed to instill this balance in my children.

One big question bothered us a lot. Why did fear play such a central role for so many in raising their kids? Then as now, Christian parents were afraid of seduction, bad ideas, and the prospect of their kids walking away from the church. These are real issues, and they deserve our serious consideration. We know we live in enemy territory and that "the whole world lies in the power of the evil one" (1 John 5:19). We know there is dark power in the universe and that the enemy of souls is intelligent, active, and brutal (Ephesians 6:12). The challenge remains for us to distinguish between healthy caution and vigilance on the one hand and reactionary fear and paranoia on the other. A distorted fear may lead to ignorance or outright hostility, but it certainly won't engender virtue. Virtue requires awareness, and awareness requires discernment.

One of the lamentable byproducts of the fear-protects mindset is its increasingly heavy-handed attempts at control for many parents. If we think that a campaign of constant surveillance and scrutiny will strengthen our kids' convictions, we'll be in for a rude awakening. Likewise, a full roster of youth events, church camps, Bible studies, mission trips, and spiritual retreats will also do little to soften a hardened heart. Neither saturation nor separation fosters spiritual maturity. I do not mean to mock or disdain the use of many of these things, which have both value and their place. But they're not fail-safe methods for spiritual indoctrination. The key issue remains formation.

Let's call to mind once more the three misguided mindsets that undermine spiritual maturity in so many homes: Instead of cultivating wisdom and discernment, we often work to instill an abiding sense of fear and suspicion of the surrounding culture (fear protects). Likewise, by placing all the emphasis on the right doctrine, scriptural knowledge, and information (information saves), we betray naive anthropology that construes human beings as being defined by what they think rather than what they love. When we encounter the limitations of information, however, we often outsource our children's spiritual education in the hopes that some specialist can repair their damaged convictions (spiritual education belongs to experts).

All of these mindsets ignore or seriously neglect questions that ought to be answered in the home. Left unanswered, these concerns can then become the roots of doubt. Elaborating on the thinking in his book *God in the Dark*, I once heard Os Guinness say, "Doubt is a halfway house between faith and unbelief."[6] If we take time as parents to address the doubts our kids are dealing with, it can result in a strengthened and mature faith.

Both Cameron and I have asked struggling parents whether their homes are *question-safe zones*. Are certain topics simply banished? If we avoid our kids' questions or, worse, if our kids don't even feel the freedom to raise them in the first place, they'll seek other sources of authority to guide them. Other sources and alternatives to the gospel are readily available, and it's all too easy to find competing ideas and narratives that answer these doubts. The stakes are high.

LETTING OUR GOOD WORKS SHINE BEFORE OUR KIDS

When my kids were small, most of their questions popped up right before bed. Like many young boys, Cameron was deeply curious about his dad's past. Rather than conceal the sordid details, I wanted both kids to know that I had once lived as a spiritual rebel. I began by telling Cameron a story of a bad man who was angry and who fought constantly with his parents and then left home to do his own thing. I outlined some of this man's journey and his determination to live without limits—to live for his own pleasures and will. Cameron was engrossed. I then told him that the bad man was me. I explained how Christ had come into my life, changed me in my inmost being, and how I then sought to follow him. I wanted him to understand that God was not a mere idea to me; he was not a concept, nor was Christianity a moral system to be outwardly conformed to. When I met the Lord of all creation, the result was not spiritual expertise; it was transformation. It all centered on the reality of the living God and his will and purpose for us all. It was a faith that had to be personal and encountered, not mimicked and performed.

To this day Cameron maintains that this was his first genuine encounter with a transformed life. Notice that he didn't have to travel countless miles to a conference or youth retreat to hear a celebrated expert. He simply laid in bed and listened to his dad tell him of the wonders of his salvation.

I have suggested three crucial pursuits as an antidote to the irrational fear on display in so many Christian homes. First, loving God supremely and making him the center of all your pursuits. Second, cultivating wisdom and discernment in the household rather than reactionary fear. Finally, modeling fidelity to Christ and his Word with consistency so our kids "may see [our] good works and give glory to [our] Father who is in heaven" (Matthew 5:16). Our devotion must move from a limited domain of the church and religious activities to the place where all of life is seen as the "theater of God's glory," to use John Calvin's phrase. This vision requires that we work deeply and internally on our attitudes and our orientation. Seeking satisfaction and contentment in God is a crucial, lifelong pursuit.

Wisdom is a central feature of scriptural teaching. Psalms, Proverbs, Ecclesiastes, and Job provide deep pools of insight that should be gleaned, known, and translated into daily life. Our witness then is the visible expression of these truths taken seriously and lived out before God and others. It is summed up in Jesus's reminder in Matthew 5:13-16:

> You are the salt of the earth, but if salt has lost its taste, how shall its saltiness be restored? It is no longer good for anything except to be thrown out and trampled under people's feet.
>
> You are the light of the world. A city set on a hill cannot be hidden. Nor do people light a lamp and put it under a basket, but on a stand, and it gives light to all in the house. In the same way, let your light shine before others, so that they may see your good works and give glory to your Father who is in heaven.

Challenging? Yes! But we are far from alone: "Not by might, nor by power, but by my Spirit, says the LORD of hosts" (Zechariah 4:6).

5

CULTIVATING LOVE

*"Teacher, which is the great commandment in the Law?" And
he said to him, "You shall love the Lord your God with all your
heart and with all your soul and with all your mind. This
is the great and first commandment. And a second is like
it: You shall love your neighbor as yourself. On these two
commandments depend all the Law and the Prophets."*

MATTHEW 22:36-40

A young Christian pastor and leader faced a real dilemma. He
loved the gospel, he loved the church, he loved ministry, and
he wanted to serve. But things had turned grim in his country.
Religious liberty was being restricted. The political climate was
growing steadily more ominous. Churches were being tightly moni-
tored, and pastors were being warned to keep their teaching as
innocuous as possible, lest they arouse the suspicions of the au-
thorities. This young leader was on the radar as a possible threat.

Friends from abroad, knowing of the rapidly deteriorating situation in his homeland and his gifts as a scholar, offered him an academic position and fresh opportunities in a far-away country. He
could study, write, preach, and serve without facing any of the
hostilities of his own nation. His writings and talents could still
serve his people, even from a distance, but without the threats and

distractions. He accepted the offer, set his affairs in order, said his goodbyes to family and friends, and sailed to the United States. He arrived to a warm welcome and took quickly to the open doors and opportunities presented to him.

However, our young pastor, Dietrich Bonhoeffer, grew increasingly conflicted. He reflected on the many Christians still laboring in what was then Nazi Germany. He thought of his initial call and desire to serve the German people, and he began to feel guilty and grieved that he had left them behind to struggle and suffer, even as he was now free from such cares. As time went by, his deep love for God, for truth, for the gospel, and for the German people decided the case for him. He would go back. When he told those who had welcomed him to America of his decision, he was met with shock and fervent protests. Had he lost his mind? Was he not paying attention to the news? The political situation was escalating and showed no signs of reversing. But Bonhoeffer did return. It was a decision that eventually cost him his life. His earlier desire for what was expedient, seemingly wise, or best for himself was overruled by his deeper sense of what was ultimately right before the Lord. A higher love overruled the selfish love that would elevate self-preservation above self-sacrifice.

In Matthew 22:36-40, Jesus responds to a lawyer's question about the greatest commandment. It's one of the rare occasions when Christ offers a straightforward answer: he tells this legal expert that we must first love the Lord our God with all that we are (heart, soul, mind, and strength). But then he expands on his answer by telling his interlocutor that the second greatest commandment is to love one's neighbor as oneself. The sequence here is crucial. Only if you love the Lord your God with all that you are will you be able to love others as yourself. Trying to love others selflessly on your own strength is an exercise in futility. Scripture is crystal clear that "we love because he first loved us" (1 John 4:19). Our Lord's primal act of love inaugurates our own relational capacities, and this same love liberates us to prioritize others—to take up our crosses and lay down our lives for the sake of the world.

As a young Christian I had missed the point about the centrality of love in the Christian life. It was there in so many passages, hidden in plain sight. How did I miss it? One reason is an all-too-common mistake in our Western and North American churches: I had been trained to think that the most important issue was the accuracy of my beliefs and that my priority consisted in securing the correct information. Without realizing it I had deeply absorbed the idea that information saves. If we were to update Christ's commands to reflect the assumptions of so many of our churches, they might read like something along the lines of you shall *understand* the Lord your God with all your mind. And the second is like it. You shall teach your neighbor all that they must *know* about the Lord.

These kinds of renderings always risk oversimplification and caricature, so hear me carefully. I am not denigrating the life of the mind. Indeed, as an apologist I'm consistently highlighting the fact that Christ includes the mind in his supreme command! Along with 1 Peter 3:15-16, Paul also exhorts us to be transformed by the renewing of our minds (Romans 12:2) and to "take every thought captive to obey Christ" (2 Corinthians 10:5). I'm also keenly aware of the importance of knowledge in the Christian life. In Hosea 4:6 the prophet gives voice to the Lord's indictment,

> My people are destroyed for lack of knowledge;
>> because you have rejected knowledge,
>> I reject you from being a priest to me.
> And since you have forgotten the law of your God,
>> I also will forget your children.

As Dallas Willard argues, "Belief cannot reliably govern life and action except in its proper connection with knowledge and with the truth and evidence knowledge involves."[1]

At the same time, we can't overlook the relational nature of the knowledge Hosea is talking about. The Lord's accusation carries tremendous force because his people don't know him personally; they have no relationship with him. It's the same travesty that underlies the chilling verses in Matthew 7:21-23:

> Not everyone who says to me, "Lord, Lord," will enter the kingdom of heaven, but the one who does the will of my Father who is in heaven. On that day many will say to me, "Lord, Lord, did we not prophesy in your name, and cast out demons in your name, and do many mighty works in your name?" And then will I declare to them, "I never *knew* you; depart from me, you workers of lawlessness." (Emphasis added.)

Our knowledge of our heavenly Father is predicated on our love for him, not on our knowledge *about* him. Plenty of non-Christian academics, for instance, know more *about* Christianity than the faithful believers who gather in the pews each Sunday. They may have written countless articles and books on Christ's incarnation and could run circles around us on the history of the early church. But it would also be entirely accurate to say that they don't truly know Christ at all. They know a lot about him, in the same way that an art historian knows a lot about Henri Matisse. C. S. Lewis makes an important distinction between the initial "assent to a proposition" (e.g., that God exists) and the culminating "adherence to *this* God": "You are no longer faced with an argument which demands your assent, but with a Person who demands your confidence."[2] Yes, knowing about God is crucial, but we cannot know him in the deepest sense until we have first given him our hearts. This is the practical reality of love's priority in the Christian life.

Why is the heart so central? As Dallas Willard says, "The human heart, will, or spirit is the executive center of human life. The heart is where decisions and choices are made for the whole person."[3] Here we find a clear picture of the frequent discrepancy between words and actions. If someone claims to follow Jesus but leads a life of unremitting selfishness, it's clear that their hearts are captive to something else. In Jesus' own words, "This people honors me with their lips, but their heart is far from me" (Matthew 15:8).

Indeed, a convincing public display of honoring the Lord with our lips frequently requires a high degree of training and theological accuracy. Since we place such a high premium on intellectual achievement, we tend to celebrate people who are skilled at publicly honoring the Lord. This focus on the sheen of a gospel presentation is one of the peculiar marks of Christian celebrity culture. Theological accuracy is important, of course, but it doesn't guarantee genuine faith. Sadly, our cultural moment is punctuated by a growing roster of accomplished church leaders whose offstage lives tell a story that's profoundly at odds with their professed convictions. As disconcerting as it sounds, it's entirely possible to master Christian discourse without giving one's heart to Jesus. This is why our Lord makes it clear that we can't afford to be naive about the primacy of love in our lives. The mark of a true disciple remains a surrendered heart.

BEGINNING BY ADDRESSING THE HEART

Despite the waning influence of the church in the United States, the nation still retains a good deal of its Christian heritage. When we moved to the Bible Belt South in 1998, I was unprepared for the challenge of cultural Christianity. Though I remained unmoved by the glossy appeals of Christian celebrity culture and the duplicity of seeing the church as nothing more than a social club, I began to notice some alarming symptoms in Cameron. As a product of a missionary household, he remained adept at giving lip service to the gospel—the only requirement for many people around us. But

I lived with him and didn't have the luxury of taking him at his word. His attitude had gone from sullen to downright hostile, and his interest in all things outré was now degenerating into a growing fascination with the occult. Part of me was deeply confused. As someone who had fled the ravages of a life without Christ, I knew firsthand the stark difference between the man I once had been and the man I had become. To carry on some sort of spiritual charade in order to lead a double life made no sense to me. But my son was a master at fooling those around him. Worst of all, he was beginning to fool himself—to believe his own lies.

The fear-protects mindset would have clear protocol here: seize control and monitor all of the child's actions, confiscate any offending items, and place tight strictures on all future activities. As we've seen, another strategy is to replace what's been erased: fill the calendar with "spiritual activities" like church camps, youth events, and conferences. While these resources have their place, they remain powerless before a hardened heart. The Lord alone has authority in this treacherous region.

So what do we do? Am I offering a counsel of despair? By no means. We may not have control over our child's heart, but we do have the ability to *address* the child's heart rather than the head alone. Cameron wasn't lacking in information; he was lacking in devotion. He knew all the right answers regarding his faith, but his actions—the underlying motivations of his life—told a completely different story. In the sobering words of James, "faith by itself, if it does not have works, is dead" (James 2:17). Cameron will fill in the details in his biographical interlude, but I knew that his heart was not surrendered to Christ, and so I decided to address my question to his heart.

To return to a pivotal morning that comes up repeatedly in this book because it was such a watershed moment, I turned to my son as he was making breakfast before school one day and asked him,

"Why do you call yourself a Christian?" Notice that I didn't ask him what he thought about Christianity or whether he understood it. Again, those are important questions, but I wanted to hear why he lived the way he did—I wanted him to deal with his actions, not his words. Though the question angered him at the time—heart questions are prone to do that—it proved instrumental in turning his life around. To this day Cameron names this as one of the most important moments in the recovery of his faith. I must confess that at the time it simply felt like another strained conversation that ended on an abrupt note.

Nothing quite prepares us for the spiritual challenge of seeing our kids flounder in their relationship with Christ. To make matters worse, there is no fail-safe formula, no expert, no conference, no podcast that can preclude or resolve this struggle. There is, however, the vital perspective of recognizing the primacy of love in human life, and we would do well to begin by addressing the heart.

In Luke 18, Jesus encounters a rich young ruler who is eager to learn the secret of eternal life: "Good Teacher, what must I do to inherit eternal life?" (v. 18). Jesus immediately cuts to the heart of the matter by asking why the man calls him good, since "God alone is good." The question is testing this man's actual convictions concerning Jesus. As we've seen, it's one thing to view Jesus as a "good teacher" and quite another to do what he says. Jesus then gives an overview of the commands, and the rich young ruler affirms that he keeps them all. With penetrating spiritual insight Jesus then addresses this man's heart directly: "One thing you still lack. Sell all that you have and distribute to the poor, and you will have treasure in heaven; and come, follow me" (v. 22). Deeply saddened, the man walks away (v. 23). This man's immense wealth outweighed his devotion to Christ.

The problem was not one of understanding but rather of the heart. Treasure in heaven could not compete with his earthly treasure. We see a marked contrast later in the same chapter when Peter points to the fact that all of the disciples have given up everything to follow Jesus, a clear sign of their authentic devotion. Christ responds, "Truly, I say to you, there is no one who has left house or wife or brothers or parents or children, for the sake of the kingdom of God, who will not receive many times more in this time, and in the age to come eternal life" (vv. 29-30). Our devotion to Christ may well set us at odds with our very family members, but if our hearts belong to him, we must forsake all for his sake.

During these trials of faith within our households, may I suggest that we follow our Lord's advice by first addressing the hearts of our children? By doing so, we will push them to move beyond what they say they know and help them to deal with what they believe. They may not appreciate it, but addressing the heart removes the luxury of self-denial.

A JOURNEY OF THE HEART

I began at ground zero at my conversion. This spiritual immaturity stood in marked contrast to my wife, Mary, who had grown up in a Catholic home in the United States and had given her life to Christ when she was introduced to the gospel in a Bible study during her teenage years. She went on to study missions in college—an experience that fostered in her an abiding love of God's Word. Despite our different backgrounds, when we met we were both committed to the radical lifestyle and calling of mission and faithfulness that we saw in Scripture, and both of us sought to build our lives on God's Word and his way. Our imaginations were fired by the life of Christ, the call to be disciples, and the demand to follow his call to the ends of the earth. This call took us from our respective native lands to Vienna, Austria, where we lived for over twenty years.

We embraced the call to serious nonconformity to the spirit and mood of our age. We wanted to be different, to be focused, to be committed. John Stott captures the spirit of our endeavors in his book *The Radical Disciple*: "Here then is God's call to a radical discipleship, to a radical nonconformity to the surrounding culture. It is a call to develop a Christian counterculture, a call to engagement without compromise."[4]

Young and zealous, we were part of a vibrant community that sought to seriously follow God's Word in exploring simple living and service. Our mission stressed dedication to the advance of the gospel, and it nurtured a committed attempt to embody the truth as faithfully as we could. George Verwer, who founded OM in the 1960s, sought to do whatever was necessary to advance the gospel. His dedication soon attracted hundreds of students who wanted to be a part of the movement. They fanned out into many countries, particularly those who were unreached or resistant to the gospel. The team Mary and I joined was called the Greater Europe team and was focused on the communist countries of Central and Eastern Europe.

Looking back, I can now describe my spiritual journey as a journey of the heart. I was launched into a sea of change. I had made a clean break from my former way of life. In stark contrast to the hyper-individualistic pursuit of freedom that characterized my early years, I was now being instructed by the Gospels on the servant love of Christ, and I was seeing firsthand that self-denial is at the center of daily living. The diversity on display in God's kingdom also confronted me with another challenge: I was learning what it meant to work in ethnically, denominationally, economically, and socially diverse teams. Dealing with sin and relational tensions, denying self, and actively seeking to serve others—these were not simply spiritual aspirations but essential ingredients for doing the Lord's work.

Most galling was the fact that taking up one's cross was not limited to our evangelistic endeavors. I had to take care of those around me, including the annoying people who kept raiding my closet and borrowing my shirts. One gentleman had the habit of grinning and simply saying, "Brother, I felt the liberty."

In *The Screwtape Letters*, C. S. Lewis inserts these cunning words into the mouth of his senior devil:

> Think of your man as a series of concentric circles, his will being the innermost, his intellect coming next, and finally his fantasy. You can hardly hope, at once, to exclude from all the circles everything that smells of the Enemy: but you must keep on shoving all the virtues outward till they are finally located in the circle of fantasy, and all the [vices] inward into the Will. It is only in so far as [the virtues] reach the Will and are there embodied in habits that [they] are really fatal to us.[5]

The first task in serving others is learning to serve the people right in front of you. A consistent strategy of the enemy is to move your neighbor to the realm of fantasy, or, better still, to an anonymous crowd or audience. Though there's nothing wrong with a public ministry, the stage imposes a distance that's often exploited by the enemy. It's in this sense that many highly effective evangelists with thriving ministries expend all their energy on strangers in a crowd while neglecting the people closest to them.

I cannot imagine a more realistic or practical setting to test a person's commitment to love than those early days on the mission field. Nothing will reveal your commitment to servanthood quite like shared living space. Love for God was tied clearly to our love for one another in the biblical vision: "By this all people will know that you are my disciples, if you have love for one another" (John 13:35). Verwer and the other leaders of OM were very clear about the practical implications of love. There is nothing like shared work and deadlines to test the mettle and hearts of all.

This lesson was vividly driven home to me when the crew of one of our OM ships was confronted with a blockage in the septic tank. These vessels greatly expanded the evangelistic reach of our organization and thus served as emblems of self-sacrifice. However, this time that self-sacrifice would take on a much more visceral connotation; the only way to fix the blockage was to climb into the tank and unclog the drain by hand. A heated argument arose about who would venture into this fetid chamber. As voices continued to rise, one of the OM leaders calmly stepped forward, suited up, and fixed the blockage. To this day I'm hard-pressed to find a more practical example of servant-hearted leadership.

I was often impressed by the lives and devotion of my brothers and sisters from other countries. One Dutch brother was an incredible example. He was a prayer warrior and a dedicated evangelist who exuded love and compassion. I well remember one exchange when he said to me, "People don't care how much you know, but they do know how much you care." At first I resisted his comment, but as time went by I came to see that this kind of loving expression was indeed at the heart of Christianity. Not love as a mere idea or moral belief but love as an embodied expression of compassion, service, and deeds on a daily basis.

James K. A. Smith offers a compelling description of how this embodied expression of our faith begins to shape us. "Christian formation is a conversion of the imagination effected by the Spirit, who recruits our most fundamental desires by a kind of narrative enchantment—by inviting us narrative animals into a story that seeps into our bones and becomes the orienting background of our being-in-the-world."[6] The daily dynamics of our team life in OM confirm Smith's words. We met every day for devotions, followed by our work assignments. Wednesday evenings were reserved for an extended time of prayer when we covered the nations with intercession. We also heard requests from OM fields and personnel from around the globe. These prayer meetings often began at 7:30 p.m. and stretched into the wee hours of the morning. We were being trained to see and value what was most essential in life and in God's kingdom.

But my incipient devotion was often equal parts sincere and comical. On one occasion I went to an evening get-together for singles. Primed for an intense night of Bible sharing, testimonies, worship, and prayer, I was horrified to discover that we were there to watch TV! I was offended. Were we not set apart from the world? Did we not gather as his people for his purposes? Why this descent into secular carnality? In protest I sat behind a sofa and read my Bible until the time came for us to go home. What I lacked in maturity I more than made up for in sincerity. One young lady in particular greeted my courageous devotion with a sardonic smile, and our subsequent years of marriage have not erased the hilarity of this incident for her; Mary still laughs every time it's mentioned. I had much to learn—and much to unlearn.

I eventually got over my aversion to movies, and I've since stopped doing my devotions behind other people's couches at parties. It was in these more mature years that I encountered Roland Joffé's film *The Mission*. The character played by Robert De Niro, Rodrigo Mendoza, is a slave trader in the 1740s selling the Guarani people of northeastern Argentina to nearby plantations. After killing his brother in a fight over a lover, he is racked by guilt and sorrow and seeks to atone for his sins. He enlists the help of the missionary to the Guarani people, Father Gabriel (played by Jeremy Irons).

In a justly celebrated scene, he is climbing a cliff face beside a waterfall. To do penance for his former mercenary career, he carries a massive burden filled with his weapons and armor, the tools of his trade. A ragged effigy of his former self, we see him staggering over the treacherous terrain with fierce determination, his body caked in mud. He has worn himself down and his energy is gone. Finally, when he's on the verge of collapse, a Guarani tribesman approaches him with a dagger. He freezes and awaits his fate, keenly aware that he is responsible for destroying so many of these people's lives. The man brings the dagger to his neck but then pulls it away and cuts the rope holding the massive burden. He then flings it into the river where it quickly sinks from view. Like Christian in the *Pilgrim's Progress*, Mendoza is liberated, set free. He begins to weep as the rest of the natives gather around him, touching and embracing him.

It remains one of the more compelling pictures of redemption in modern cinema. The movie then goes on to chart his journey into faith, but this journey remains a battle for his heart. Toward the conclusion of the movie he is once again tempted to pick up arms, this time to fight in defense of the Guarani people. The film doesn't offer pat answers. Father Gabriel, driven by his vision of Christ's greatest commands, is willing to lay down his life, not just for the Guarani people but also for their oppressors. Mendoza, driven by his sense of injustice, is willing to take up the sword again to fight for those he had once exploited. Whatever we believe about the rightness or wrongness of these men's choices, the film offers a powerful demonstration of the primacy of our hearts in all that we do.

How do we form our hearts in such a way that we are guided by a vision, a way of life, and a set of practices that shape us into the kind of people Christ calls us to be? In John 15:13, Jesus tells us, "Greater love has no one than this, that someone lay down his life for his friends." This sacrificial love is the unique contribution of the gospel. It is in stark contrast to the modern vision of self-indulgence, self-fulfillment, and self-expression, all of which put selfishness front and center. The problem for many of us is that our Christian models are often merely baptized versions of what the culture offers, while the radical demands of the love that God's character reveals and that God offers are neglected, ignored, or reframed to suit modern tastes, preferences, and sensibilities.

If we want families that follow Christ, then we need to nurture this love in our homes and make sure everything we do is an expression of it. If we find ourselves or our family members faltering in this crucial endeavor, we would do well to begin by following our Lord's example and addressing the heart.

6

PUTTING ON CHRIST

If then you have been raised with Christ, seek the things that are
above, where Christ is, seated at the right hand of God. Set your
mind on things that are above, not on the things that are on earth.
For you have died, and your life is hidden with Christ in God.

COLOSSIANS 3:1-3

The modern world is shaped by a hunger for order and technique. The basic story bequeathed to us by the Enlightenment is that human beings are rational creatures in control of their own destiny. From pop culture to history classes to self-help seminars, this implicit narrative is fed to most of us from our earliest days. We've all internalized it and are thoroughly shaped by it. We are taught to seek knowledge, to look for practical solutions to all of life's problems, and to learn how to set goals, make plans, and deploy resources to well-honed ends.

In practical terms this means we want professionals and experts to tackle life's challenges. But the impact of these ideas has moved way beyond improving efficiencies in the marketplace. Our infatuation with technique has come to infiltrate all aspects of our lives, including the spiritual.

Driven by the tendency to specialization and optimization, formal training is routinely prioritized over character and spirituality, and professional expertise takes the place of spiritual maturity. Reflecting on our highly technical approach to Scripture, theologian Hans Boersma notes a pronounced tendency to outsource spiritual authority to experts: "Advocates of purely historical exegesis ask the reader to trust the biblical scholar. That demand removes the authority of interpretation from the Church to the academy. Not surprisingly, it is often my best students whose confidence is most shaken by this shift."[1] Sadly, the lopsided results of this emphasis are all too evident in the numerous headlines of highly gifted church leaders whose behavior betrays a grossly underdeveloped spiritual life.

Hear me carefully: I am not denigrating education and formal training. Rather, I'm arguing that spiritual maturity is not a by-product of technique but rather the fruit of steadfast devotion to Christ in all aspects of our lives. To think that such an undertaking can be accomplished through earning degrees and certificates is simply a category mistake. As we've already seen, it's possible to have a prodigious knowledge of Christianity without belonging to Christ. There are plenty of examples of this phenomenon in the theology departments of some of our most influential colleges.

If we view the church as a place of professional spirituality, then we may find ourselves seeking to outsource to the experts all the struggles to be faced in the normal hustle and bustle of family life and thereby undermine our responsibility to minister to one another (Ephesians 4:15). The church gets viewed as a kind of service center for input, therapy, and childcare. The priesthood of all believers—a central idea recaptured at the Reformation—becomes the priesthood of *some* believers, but really only those who are properly qualified. We the consumers turn to the experts and the professionals to provide the needed spiritual services. If you're a parent, however, this tendency runs the risk of undermining both your authority and your spiritual responsibility to the young lives entrusted to you by the Lord. Though our deep love for our children often drives us to consult the experts, the fact remains that none of our faults and shortcomings stopped the Lord from making us parents.

My experiences as a young Christian form a striking contrast to this atmosphere of slick professionalism that I sometimes see today. Evangelized by a young and recently married couple, I was a regular fixture at their home. They were neither the most gifted of communicators nor were they formally trained in theology. None of that stopped them from allowing me to raise numerous questions in their home, even when they didn't know the answer. They would listen intently and then open their Bibles and begin to show me what Scripture had to say to my questions. We would often talk up to a point where it became essential to pray and ask God to do what only he could do. I valued the sense that there was a fluid and living dynamic in this pursuit. It was not simply a question of looking up a set of rules or consulting a manual on how to live better. I was being included and apprenticed to a new way of life. The transmission of core values, beliefs, and practices was essential to the outcome and was modeled for me in the vibrant lives of my teachers.

Looking back, it's possible to highlight some of the essential features in the process of my nurture and formation. First, their home was a sanctuary—a locus of fellowship, conviviality, fun, education, honest interaction, and accountability. Things can be done in a home that no other space allows. I was a spiritual child in the home of my newfound spiritual parents, but what about your own kids? Is your home the kind of place where their questions are welcomed? Or do you simply defer to the "experts"? Do you place a moratorium on difficult topics?

I once spoke with a college student whose dad had forbidden any discussion of the problem of evil. When I asked him why, he replied,

"It's the reason my older brother's an atheist, so Dad figures it's not a safe topic." It's true; evil isn't a safe topic. But neither is muzzling any further conversation on the matter. Such a maneuver is evasive at best and downright irresponsible at worst. Of all the places to have these trying discussions with your kids, your home offers the safest and most conducive environment.

As paralyzing as our shortcomings can feel, we need to recover a robust reliance on the Holy Spirit as we seek the Lord's guidance in these conversations. This may include careful research on our part. If our kids ask difficult questions, we need to put in the work. We also need to push past the fearful stereotypes that stymy our efforts. The dreaded "atheist professor" has attained a position in some Christian homes that's close to a Michael Myers or a Freddy Krueger. Any professor, atheist or otherwise, is obligated to challenge their students. If your kids come from a home where they see the vibrancy of life in Christ, they'll be prepared for robust discussions in the classroom.

Though the notion that Christianity has a distinctive culture was foreign to me at the time of my conversion, I immediately began to see and feel the difference between God's kingdom and the chaotic world I'd come from. In sharp contrast to the world I'd known, Christians were primarily defined by *whose* they were rather than who they thought they were. Unlike those outside the church, Christians know they aren't men and women in control of their own destiny. Rather, their destiny is in the hands of the living God.

My former friends from Glasgow's criminal underworld would have unleashed a torrent of profanity before reaching for their knives and balling up their fists if anyone hinted that their destiny was in someone else's hands. Their ruthless script had room for nothing more than selfish ambition. When I met with my new Christian friends, however, the culture was one of nurture, learning, and mutual support—not unlike the recovery circles of Alcoholics Anonymous. (I'll let Cameron tell you about that.) I learned that life was a serious business and that everything from the most momentous events down to the most quotidian details mattered intensely. I learned that God is interested in the small stuff and the big stuff. How fitting that our Lord chose to commemorate his sacrificial death for us not with some extravagant display but with the simple bread and cup.

It was ingrained in my early Christian life that God was at the heart of life and that we were to actively and continuously seek him with the expectation that he would lead us and use us. In this sense there were no special people and no little ones. God could use any of us—the only issue was our availability and response, not our qualifications. I learned a lot from observing the lives of the elders of my church. Several of these were former coal miners, men used to hard and dangerous work. In prayer meetings the speech of these rugged men overflowed with verses from the vast portions of Scripture they had memorized, as well as imagery from the scores of hymns they had committed to memory. It was hard not to picture them in the maw of the earth, blackened with soot, singing these timeless hymns in their raspy voices. None of them were highly educated, and they would have scoffed at the idea of spiritual experts, yet they were deeply proficient in the life of the Spirit.

In my journey to OM, I experienced another level of this kind of life. We were challenged to hear God's Word afresh. We were challenged to consider the serious call it brought to discover firsthand what it means to "seek first the kingdom of God and his righteousness" (Matthew 6:33). The centrality, urgency, and importance of that mission were made clear, not simply as an idea but as an essential focus and practice. The young couple and others I met truly modeled this practice. They began their days in prayer. They sought God actively and in his Word. They were on the lookout for opportunities to serve, share, and help throughout the day. They concluded each day with prayer and thanksgiving. Coming from the self-centered and impulsive world I had been in, the impact of this completely new way of life was profound. The differences, as Guinness would say in another context, made a difference.

In an address to our OM team on the Doulos ship (one of OM's two ships) in the fall of 1978, I heard the old preacher Alan Redpath say, "Some of us are more afraid of the Holy Spirit than we are of sin." As trinitarian Christians, it is surprising how, for some of us, the Holy Spirit plays little or no role in our thinking or in our conscious living. Jesus taught us in John 16 that it was to our advantage that he go away so that the Spirit would come. This *life in the Spirit* is central to our way in the home and our interaction as family. If one of the demanding and insistent challenges of modernity and secularization is the tendency to focus on the immanent and the immediate, then teaching and nurturing a true understanding and practice of transcendence is vital. I mean this not in some impersonal, detached, or merely cognitive way. I mean a true spirituality of communion, encounter, and engagement, not with concepts but with God himself.

As a family we had a great illustration of God's intervening grace during some of our harder years in the teenage phase. Cameron is a talented musician and played in a band, like so many disaffected suburban kids with little athletic talent. As part of this journey he had saved up and bought an expensive bass guitar. He loved that guitar and jamming with his friends. One weekend they decided to enter into a local battle of the bands. It was a big event held at the Mall of Georgia. Cameron and his band duly entered, played their slot, and then Cameron absconded with his then-girlfriend, thinking they failed to make an impression. He was wrong. Unknown to Cameron, his band had won first place and his bandmates were desperately looking for him. And in the rush of it all he had left his guitar at the mall in public view.

When he later discovered his mistake and went back to the mall to check on his guitar, it was gone. He was angry at himself for this carelessness, but the instrument seemed lost for good. Mary was at that time leading a Bible study for several women from our church. One of them, Robyn, a neighbor from across the street, heard the story and was grieved by it. As mundane as the situation seemed they all knew how important music was in Cameron's life, and they prayed that God would work. One day Robyn was walking down a corridor in the school where she taught. She overheard some kids talking about a bass guitar that another kid had found at the mall. She introduced herself to the group who cheerfully referred her to the new owner of the bass.

She introduced herself and asked about the guitar. A garbled story was told about finding it at the mall, and she explained whose it was and where it came from. The young man happily handed the instrument over. She took it back and said she would return it. She called Mary to ask if Cameron was home. Mary affirmed he was, and Robyn said, "Keep him there, I have a surprise." Robyn had been praying and expected the Holy Spirit would lead her. When she rang our doorbell, we asked Cameron to answer it. Robyn was ecstatic. She shared the story, her prayers, God's leading, and how she knew this was the Lord. She gave Cameron his rescued guitar and told him first to never doubt the Lord's love and grace and to remember this moment. This whole experience touched us all and was a sterling reminder of God's care in everyday life. The bass sits in Cameron's office to this day.

I want to draw attention again to some of the components involved here. We see the role of the home and how God moves in the domestic and mundane as much as anywhere else. Robyn's heart and her habits were attuned to God and practiced in both seeking God's intervention and on expecting him to work. The way she handled the process, including the phone call, waiting to surprise Cameron, and feeling the thrill of what God was doing, was an object lesson of how life can be attuned to God and his ways. While Robyn knew her prayers didn't guarantee the recovery of the bass, she also understood that the Lord is active in every facet of our lives, and her simple, childlike sense of expectation is a lesson to all of us. None of this demanded some kind of superspirituality or a special kind of person or qualities. It was simply paying heed to the ways God works, the resources he gives, and exercising faith and trust in the daily happenings of life.

Encountering God and expecting him in the everyday is vital to forming our lives in Christ. If we never speak practically of God's presence, if we never seek him or consult him in our homes, we are communicating that God is only in the church or in so-called sacred spaces but largely absent in the living room, the bedroom, and the kitchen. We can unconsciously teach the family a form of functional atheism or a form of deism—the idea that God is a distant technician who set creation in motion and now remains uninterested in the daily circumstances of our lives.

In my own experience missionary families offered the clearest picture of Christian expectation. They depended on God for just about all of their practical affairs: visas, finances to cover their needs and operations, proficiency with a foreign language and culture, and success in reaching the lost. Many who have nurtured glorious visions of evangelism in the streets of a distant nation experience a profoundly rude awakening as they stroll down the opaque aisles of a foreign grocery store and negotiate a public transport system that's as convoluted as it is immense. To remain in this context for the long haul requires more than determination; it requires the three primal Christian virtues of faith, hope, and love. As exotic as this orientation may sound, none of it should be viewed as special, even for those of us who make our homes in the quiet suburbs of more affluent nations. In fact, this sense of foreignness is the new normal for Christian disciples. First Peter 2:11 describes us *all* as "strangers and pilgrims" (KJV), and it seems to me that understanding this is a central aspect of being a part of the Christian community.

In an inversion of the old spiritual, it is as if many of us would prefer to sing, "*This* world is my home, I am (not) passing through." In other words, the expectations, goals, priorities, and values most important to us are those defined by contemporary culture, not by God's Word, our tradition, or the demands of mission. We live exclusively for the here and now. Our desires, expectations, and imaginations are fired solely by the immanent. The eternal and the transcendent are consigned to the realm of consoling fantasy, uplifting stories designed for sympathy cards. The crucial question remains: are our lives our own? Are we free to choose our destiny? Or is there a sense in which calling shapes us and defines us? Consider this definition of call from Os Guinness: "Calling is the truth that God calls us to Himself so decisively that everything we are, everything we do, and everything we have is invested with a special devotion and dynamism lived out as a response to his summons and service."[2]

A challenge to all families comes from the need to discern the nature of your expectations—the hopes and wishes that animate your household. Once again, this is not solely a question of values, correct doctrine, and sound intellectual convictions. We need to remember that the surrounding culture makes its appeal to us primarily as lovers, not thinkers.

In our annual family cycle, the Christmas season in Austria provided a lot of special times for us to not only celebrate but to enter deeply into our greater Christian narrative and its meaning. Austria is a Catholic nation and takes the Christmas season seriously. For the most part Santa Claus is mercifully absent. Instead, children are introduced to St. Nicholas at an early age. Though Austria is now largely secular, this time of year brings an immense wealth of the church's imagery. Snow tops the gothic roofs of the ancient cathedrals as their sanctuaries ring with choirs singing timeless hymns. Our family would gather around the advent wreath (*kranz*) to light the four candles that anticipate the coming of the Savior. We used these times and these moments in the yearly cycle to tell the gospel story, to talk of the real meaning of Christmas and the Savior. In contrast with the hollow commercialism that replaces the joy of Christian expectation for so many, our kids learned from an early age what it means to anticipate the coming of our Lord.

For most of the year, however, it's all too easy to push our faith to the margins, even though we come from a tradition that centers the entire year on the life, death, and resurrection of Christ. Apart from the harm to our spiritual well-being is the danger of imparting this same fragmentation to our children. Once internalized a compartmentalized faith in Christ is deeply insidious and quietly undermines any serious commitment. If Christ is nothing less than the infinite Son of God, the Savior of the world, the Lord of all creation, it makes no sense to argue that we can outgrow him. Compartmentalized faith, however, is easily outgrown because a close examination soon reveals it to be empty. You can't outgrow Christ, but you can and should outgrow a caricature.

The contemporary Western church seems to offer a two-tier approach to faith. Option one is what I call "Christianity Lite," which is for the everyman and covers those who can do or cope with the bare minimum and want church with little or no serious demands. Christianity Lite is for those who mistakenly believe they can have Christ on their own terms. Option two is "Christianity Heavy"—a program for spiritual overachievers who aren't content to leave their faith in the sanctuary. The distinction is wholly spurious.

Indeed, the New Testament makes no distinction between Christians and disciples. If I may rephrase the question that so disturbed my teenage son: Why do you call Christ Lord? Do your children know why you do? If we view discipleship as anything more or less than basic Christianity, we have distorted the teachings of Christ and misunderstood what it means to follow him.

True discipleship is solidly grounded in our *yes* to God and our *no* to all that hinders or stands in the way of faithfulness. In Romans 1:7, the apostle Paul writes to the Christians in Rome and instructs them that they are "loved by God" and that they are called "saints." Both directions are important and both must be taught and cultivated in our homes. Set apart *from* that which denies God and his truth, *from* that which undermines or corrupts his commands, *from* that which harms or hurts our life or that of others. Set apart *for* that which glorifies God, *for* that which pursues and seeks his kingdom and righteousness, and *for* that which brings love, truth, and hope as we seek to embody his truth and serve others.

If we take this all seriously, if we see that we have not lived intentionally and are not doing so now, then perhaps we could take some time, sit together as a couple, open our Bibles, pray together, and work through some simple questions. What vision animates our home? What is the mission of our family? What is our primary calling? These are common questions in our various workspaces, but why do we rarely institute this level of intentionality in our homes? After all, the home is one of the most primal and central institutions of any culture. To live *coram Deo*, in God's presence, under his authority, and for his glory demands focus and commitment. Let's take the time and make the effort to consider what it means to "put on Christ" daily.

Biographical Interlude

CAMERON'S STORY

Where shall I go from your Spirit?
Or where shall I flee from your presence?
If I ascend to heaven, you are there!
If I make my bed in Sheol, you are there!

PSALM 139:7-8

I n the world of Christian ministry, people are always badgering us for our story. Thus, I feel obliged to give a quick narrative of the Lord's radical intervention in my life—a kind of compressed *Pilgrim's Progress* replete with ogres and dragons. I worry that there's an unspoken assumption that the credibility of our story grows in direct proportion to the severity of our former life. I know that's often the case with me: I don't actively wish harm on anyone, of course, but I sure do cherish those ogres and dragons. How could I not? They're so *interesting*. If we've survived the ravages of addiction, crossed the Rubicon from another religion, emerged from the underbelly of crime, or pushed past the barriers of skepticism, our listener is probably going to take us much more seriously. After all, you can't argue with scars. There's a reason these kinds of testimonies are a mainstay at Christian conferences and special church services featuring guest speakers.

But what if your story isn't so exotic? What if you grew up in a Christian home, for instance, surrounded by faithful men and women who embodied the gospel with confounding consistency—men and women who didn't do you the courtesy of provoking a serious (and narratively compelling) rebellion? What if your family effectively robbed you of the luxury of a more impressive testimony?

There's a rough corollary between the perceived authenticity of the Christian with the past and the myth of the tortured artist. Do a bit of research on your favorite writer, poet, painter, or director, and you'll frequently find evidence of a deeply damaged individual. Case in point: one of my favorite writers is David Foster Wallace. Tortured? Check. Complex relationship with his mother? Check. Eccentric? You bet. Brilliant writer? That's an emphatic yes. Artistic credibility? Through the roof. Now apply this same litmus test to a cherished Christian testimony. Be honest, does the prodigality on display in the story tend to enhance the credibility of the witness? It's no surprise that most of us are drawn to tumultuous stories, of course. What is surprising, however, is the amount of faith we often put in ogres and dragons.

I'm an apologist, so the *What's your story?* question is unavoidable. Invariably, the person asking has an impressive sin résumé and is curious about the ogres and dragons I've battled myself. I've been asked for my story by former gangbangers, atheists, Muslims, Hindus, drug addicts, LGBTQ+ activists, and Wiccans, to name a few. *They should all write books*, I think to myself—and many of them have. "But enough about me," they say, crossing their legs and leaning in, "I want to hear *your* story!" I'm tempted to answer, "I've always lived blandly ever after," but my earnest, nondefensive thought is: *I don't have a story. I have no ogres and dragons. Do you know where I can find some?*

The other temptation is to tell these dragon-scarred interlocutors about my dad. After all, his story meets all the requirements of authentic Christian testimony. If ever there was a malnourished, mud-strewn prodigal walking on faltering feet to the Father's embrace, it's my dad. Why can't the gravity of his former rebellion atone for my conformity? Dad's the prodigal; I'm the missionary kid. Do the math.

Fittingly, one of the more dramatic chapters in my own story does involve my dad. The event in question took place in the kitchen of our family home. One of the recurring themes of this book is the fact that, for better or for worse, the seemingly innocuous domestic terrain of the family household is one of the most primal sites of our spiritual transformation.

Our family had relocated from Vienna, Austria, to the United States in 1998, and as the nation lurched its way toward the potentially apocalyptic revelations of Y2K, I was learning firsthand the social hazards of wearing the same T-shirt twice in a week. This frugality was a partial byproduct of my missionary background, but I soon learned that in the land of plenty such thrift was more than a wardrobe malfunction; it constituted a serious breach of etiquette. My chronic self-consciousness was compounded by the yawning cultural divide. Everybody kept hearing me say *Australia* when I told them I'd come from Austria. Where was my sexy accent? they wanted to know. Why was I so pale? I kept issuing mordant reminders that I came from the place where "the hills are alive with the sound of music." Amazingly, many of these kids didn't seem to know Austria was a country. One well-meaning girl asked my sister, without a hint of irony, whether we had access to modern forms of transportation in Austria.

Outsiders can have a kind of forbidden glamor, of course, especially if they happen to come from the wrong side of the tracks. While it's true that plenty of missionary kids *do* come from dangerous regions, the affluent nation of Austria, with its pristine ski slopes, lederhosen, and delectable milk chocolates, hardly qualified as dangerous. I had all the appeal of a nerdy foreign exchange student. Most of my peers, on the other hand, had grown up together. They remembered playground fights in kindergarten and still gossiped about former middle school power couples. Even if they did express occasional disdain for my sparse closet, most of these kids regarded me with idle curiosity at best, mild indifference at worst.

But as everybody knows, you've got to find your place in the teenage social hierarchy. And I learned very quickly that if you don't find that place soon, it gets assigned to you. I also learned that most adolescents are lazy and only too happy to go along with whatever role you've chosen for yourself. There's just one major requirement: You've got to look the part. The United States is the land of the free market and expressive individualism, and a large part of that dynamic involves shopping at the right places to secure your social standing.[1] Since I'd decided to make it easy on myself and go with the outcast role, I knew I'd be wearing lots of black clothes and possibly eyeliner. If you want to be a misfit, start with a Misfits T-shirt.

I had a big problem, though. I had no demons. The costume was one thing, but how was I going to *play* the part without the proper motivation? I was in desperate need of ogres and dragons, but my new suburban setting in the Bible Belt wasn't doing me any favors. It didn't augur well that my dad worked for one of the biggest names in the apologetics world, effectively turning me into a pastor's kid on steroids. No matter how much I wracked my brain, I just couldn't find a secret wellspring of deep psychic pain to lend an air of authenticity to the black nail polish and eyeliner. My parents had failed to inflict the kinds of flattering emotional scars that were a prerequisite for my gloomy persona. I was no Heathcliff—I wasn't even a Robert Smith. I did the only thing I thought I could; I went looking for demons.

Demon hunting wouldn't have been my chosen phrase if I was asked about my game plan here, of course. If anything was approaching a rationale, it probably involved nothing more than trying to be a bit more interesting. However, my growing obsession with various expressions of darkness in the arts (music in particular) was more than a superficial avenue to better self-expression: All was not right with the world, and these shrieking voices were expressing this primal fact with greater honesty than many of the people around me. "Birth, copulation, and death / Is this the meaning of life?"—so went the chorus of a song by the aptly named Carcass.[2] Though not all of us would have chosen such unsparing terms, my high school classmates and I certainly seemed to endorse the birth-copulation-death thesis with our behavior. As I saw it, these hopeless pursuits were usually disguised in flowery language and a pulsating beat that kept parties moving fast enough to avoid all serious thought. Carcass was simply stripping the varnish off of pop music and showing how hollow a godless life truly is. And, yes, this bleak vision was rendered through baritone guitars that chugged like industrial machinery and vocals that sounded like a snarling animal caught in a trap. It's uncompromising, but all these years later it still seems to me a more fitting expression of the despair behind mindless hedonism than the joyful pop tunes that celebrate the same thing in more buoyant terms.

My dad taught me the discernment necessary to understand what I was listening to. It's also worth noting that there were ample hints of my subversive tastes well before we moved to the United States. I remember one occasion in particular when I had left an album on the living room coffee table. Dad picked up the liner notes and, without a hint of alarm or defensiveness, gently deciphered all of the pagan and occult references of the album.

Given my European heritage, I ended up tapping into Norse mythology to bolster my gothic street cred. Lest you think this adolescent foray into Nordic territory involved some poetic trek toward *sehnsucht* (i.e., a transcendent sense of longing) à la C. S. Lewis, let me assure you that I took a typically American approach to this rich pagan terrain—one that required zero reading. I started buying loads of Scandinavian black metal. Burzum, Mayhem, Marduk, Emperor—these bands drew their inspiration from Norse mythology and divided their ideological allegiances equally between paganism, nihilism, and satanism. Plus, they were from Europe and I was from Europe, so I figured that made my devotion much more authentic.

Sporting corpse paint and outfits that made them look a bit like Vikings in bondage gear, many of these pioneers of extreme metal made good on their lyrical promises and burned churches, assaulted strangers, mutilated themselves, staged black masses, and in some cases went to prison as convicted murderers.[3] Being a mild-mannered and largely compliant kid, I did none of those things. I was no arsonist—I didn't even smoke. In fact, I never darkened the doorway of a single black metal show. But I sure did wear the heck out of those T-shirts, all of which I purchased through discreet mail-order transactions to spare my family the juvenile barrage of goat heads, inverted crosses, and pentagrams. Flannel shirts and jackets constituted my last piece of subterfuge before I arrived at school. Maybe not as brave as crowd surfing at a concert filled with people who think church buildings make for good bonfires, but these shirts sure would have incensed my folks, and that's a pretty major risk for a teenage guy trying to ply his trade as a card-carrying outsider. As I saw it, my black metal getup was my Samson's hair. Take it away and I was just a scared kid who needed to do some push-ups and get more sunshine.

Here's another typically American assumption: what I do in private—as long as it's legal—won't have any major public consequences. This is nonsense, of course, and if you want to test it, try playing some aggressive music in your car as you're driving in rush hour traffic. Not surprisingly, my newly acquired taste for music that celebrated unadulterated hatred and mayhem—much of it in a shrieking Gollum voice—began to seep into my attitude and behavior. Given my overwhelmingly shy nature and moral cowardice, most of this burgeoning hostility was directed at the people I loved the most because mistreating them entailed minimal risk to me. I knew that Mom and Dad would love me no matter how toxic my actions or speech. I'm ashamed to say that I exploited my parent's unconditional love for a season. I wasn't selling drugs and sleeping around—my warped fashion sense protected me from even the most intrepid members of the opposite sex—but my growing love of darkness was undeniable, and what I lacked in subtlety I made up for in sincerity.

Even though I'd never mustered the courage to go to a show, I somehow got it into my head that I could and would succeed as a black metal musician. Since I'd shown some aptitude as a singer, I decided to market myself as. a lead vocalist. When it comes to black metal, though, we're using the word *singer* in the loosest sense of the term. The traditional black metal singer channels their inner hyena to produce a sound that alternately evokes a wailing infant, a violent bout of illness, and the kind of shriek you might associate with an animate gargoyle. Practicing this sound made for some awkward moments when I wasn't the only person in the house, and it generally necessitated copious amounts of something hot and herbal. I know alcohol is usually associated with rock 'n' roll, but my choice of genre ensured that I usually had a cup of tea in my pale hands. I looked like I belonged in a library, not a Scandinavian fjord.

Dad persevered through these years, but his patience for my newfound aspiration to make a career of howling into the arctic winds of Norway was wearing thin. For a time he was reduced to writing me letters in an effort to avoid the explosive dynamics of some of our conversations. I'd wake up to find a neatly folded piece of paper slipped under my door like a hotel invoice. Invariably, these letters enjoined me to attack my homework with the same gusto as I attacked imaginary stages. Looking back, I can see that he was just trying to have an adult conversation with a petulant child. My mother, on the other hand, found herself playing the reluctant mediator or referee between the two of us. The family dinner table, formerly a haven of laughter and vibrant conversations, often became a tense battleground of pointed questions, pained side-glances, and adamant throat-slicing gestures. Since our family had never been big on small talk, most neutral conversational escapes were off-limits. An uncomfortable silence prevailed during our meals, and our normally loquacious family of four was reduced to sullen mastication sessions around the table.

One morning before school, I dragged myself into our kitchen for breakfast, only to find Dad seated at the table behind a fortress of books. This was a bad sign; it meant that he'd been up all night thinking. What was the subject of this particular wee-hour intensive study? None of the usual suspects: history, theology, sociology, and philosophy. Oh, no—something far worse. He'd been thinking about my future.

In my teenage years the question of my future was one of the most dangerous topics in our household, and I avoided it like the plague. On this particular morning, my goal was simple: grab a quick breakfast, avoid eye contact, and get the heck out of Dodge. But my efforts proved futile. Dad unfastened his gaze from the book in his hands, looked right at me, and asked, "Son, why do you call yourself a Christian?"

I stiffened as I reached for the toaster strudel in the freezer. "It's six in the morning, Dad. Do you think we could talk about this later?"

"Oh, that's just perfect, isn't it?" he blustered and beat a hasty retreat to the basement library. Ironically, *he* was the one who'd managed to escape this awkward exchange. I stood by the fridge, filled with rage, frantically trying to eject his question from my mind. The effort probably looked physical.

I could easily flip through my adolescent identity roster and tell you why I called myself a metalhead, a goth, a stoner, a scene kid, or emo—all options that came with easy scripts for a prospective outcast such as myself—but I couldn't tell you why I called myself a Christian. It's worth pausing to explain why the answer to this seemingly basic question about a way of life that had comprehensively defined my upbringing and day-to-day existence proved so elusive.

In his monumental work *A Secular Age*, Charles Taylor argues that one of the defining features of our culture is not necessarily its direct opposition to religion and traditional values but rather its increasing ability to accommodate a plethora of conflicting views by carving out an ever-widening space where they can sit side by side. Total visions of reality are reduced to a set of options. American awards shows are always fascinating examples of this phenomenon. Why is it that so many of our most risqué songwriters continue to "thank God" when they're handed a trophy for their efforts?

According to Taylor, this roominess in our beliefs is the actual calling card of contemporary secularism.[4] Again, if you want a rough picture of what this widening space looks like, think of streaming services like Hulu, Netflix, and Spotify. All those widely disparate titles. All those possibilities. All those options.

In this vagrant zone, it's perfectly sensible to mix and match. Electronic musician Tim Hecker offers a striking example of this tendency with his album *Love Streams*. Though Hecker's particular brand of mixing and matching involves Christianity, it could just as easily target Hinduism or Satanism. Drawing on everything

from classical choral arrangements to cutting-edge studio technology, his stated purpose is to make "pagan music that dances on
the ashes of a burnt church." The album reflects our cultural
landscape in microcosm. Disparate elements of the past are scav-
enged from the wreckage of the Western church, "sculpted" beyond
recognition and welded to modern software. The ensuing arrangement is a vast pastiche punctuated by an occasional murmur
from a long-forgotten spiritual tradition. It's the soundtrack of
uncertainty, a sonic tour of the restless late-modern mind. Hecker's
audiences may find themselves alternately moved and alarmed,
faintly overhearing a brief note of transcendence that is quickly
swallowed by the riot of competing noises.[5]

More than a provocateur, Hecker's bona fides include eight
studio albums—each uniquely experimental—as well as a PhD
from McGill University investigating the "cultural history of loud
sound from 1880–1930." He's no hack.

For Hecker, Christendom is a grab bag of musical accessories.
Whether it's a Gregorian chant or an aria by Josquin des Prez,
Hecker is only interested in the atmosphere of the piece. The spiritual heritage is discarded as irrelevant. This mindset allows him to
wrench these sacred arrangements from their native context,
dissect them in the laboratory of his studio, and market the hybrid
as a new product.

Love Streams is indicative of what I call the condition of cultural
oblivion—the odd paralysis that grips contemporary people as
they try to navigate a culture that has been reduced to a state of
pure immanence and that has blurred the boundaries between
sacred and profane. By turns sublime and ridiculous, blasphemous
and banal, this environment turns people into cultural nomads in
a wilderness of disparate imagery. Now the images of Che Guevara
and Charles Manson adorn T-shirts. Now the choral arrangements
of a devout composer become fodder for Tim Hecker's musical

collages. Now an insecure adolescent reared in a Christian household can earnestly believe that nihilism clad in corpse paint is compatible with the teachings of Christ.[6]

Living in the Bible Belt only compounded the issue for me. My former homeland of Austria is a largely secular nation that has forgotten its Christian heritage—a place where the stately cathedrals of bygone eras function more like museums than houses of worship, and where the ritual of dragging yourself out of bed and going to church on a Sunday morning is greeted with genuine curiosity.

Terms like *secular, atheist,* and *post-Christian* are academic and clinical, and they tend to distance us from the atmosphere of haunting vacancy that punctuates religious sites in postsecular Europe. No one describes this atmosphere better than Philip Larkin in his poem "Church Going." Larkin finds himself wandering into an old church and surveying its deserted interior. A principled unbeliever, Larkin is confounded by his seemingly unshakeable habit of visiting defunct churches:

> What shall we turn them into, if we shall keep
> A few cathedrals chronically on show,
> Their parchment, plate and pyx in locked cases,
> And let the rest rent-free to rain and sheep.[7]

There's a refreshing lack of spiritual ambiguity in post-Christian countries. In this environment a person either is or isn't a Christian. Nominal Christianity is a husk—not a viable option. The current vogue among many US believers for "liminal spaces"—broad interstitial zones between belief and unbelief—belies the fact that the church, however diminished, still holds a high level of influence in our culture.[8] Truly post-Christian cultures don't offer that same luxury. We haven't yet reached the time when displaced poets explore our churches like anthropologists doing fieldwork. That day may be on the horizon, but the fact that so many of our churches already resemble warehouses and shopping malls might make it more likely that they'd simply be repurposed as centers of commerce.

Ever since I'd moved to the South, though, I'd discovered that *everyone* was a Christian, no matter what they said or did. Asking someone about their Christian convictions was simply redundant. At the risk of overstatement, a person could have a voodoo altar in their living room and still lead worship at the local church. This social dynamic was one of the more insidious forms of culture shock I experienced when I crossed the pond from Europe. I'd often sit back and note the wide disparity between a person's testimony in a Wednesday youth group meeting and the revelations of their weekend escapades on Monday mornings in homeroom. If Stacy could "convert" Brandon *and* sleep with him (in the same week no less), why couldn't I offer lip service to Christ on Sunday and extol the virtues of nihilism on Monday?

At this point it should be clear that a simple charge of inconsistency in my worldview, though technically true, largely misses the point. Inconsistency is so deeply woven into the social fabric of contemporary culture that it's often seen as a virtue—a sign that you're open-minded, eclectic, tolerant. If Christianity is reduced to nothing more than one among numerous competing options, then drawing from its cultural capital while simultaneously indulging a life of unbridled hedonism is about as inconsistent as mixing ketchup and mustard or Pink Floyd's *The Dark Side of the Moon* and *The Wizard of Oz*. Tim Hecker's inconsistency didn't stop him from making *Love Streams*.

All this helps explain why I saw no conflict in importing corpse paint and misanthropy into my Christianity. If I thought of my worldview at all, I probably would have put most of the emphasis on the *my* part. It's *my* life, *my* view of the world, *my* Christianity.

A person's possessions may be morbid and unpleasant, but calling them inconsistent is just a category mistake.

Most people don't see their experience of life as a worldview, and they usually don't employ its conceptual language when they open up about their deeply held beliefs. What drew me to crude expressions of occultism and scrawny dudes in bad KISS makeup? It wasn't a worldview; it was a vision, albeit one that matched my lousy fashion sense. As juvenile as black metal can be, in its more inspired moments, it paints a Dionysian picture of wildness and untamed passion that's both primal and dangerous, and—if you happen to be a skinny third-culture kid nursing the usual cocktail of adolescent hormones—the atonal shrieking and poor man's Nietzsche of, say, Norwegian black metal band, Gorgoroth,[9] can cast a pretty powerful spell.

But this cerebral understanding of human action can be a difficult habit to break. I've got a friend who's fond of worldview maps—questionnaires meant to clarify a person's major assumptions by assigning them to a corresponding worldview—and in the context of campus ministry he likes to foist these surveys on any student who will give him the time of day. He always comes back saying the same thing: "These people are all over my map! There's just no consistency."

It gradually dawned on me that the map was the problem—not the students. Charles Taylor argues that our experience of life is less like a map and more like the deeply ingrained familiarity of our neighborhood. When it comes to the places where we live—the sights, the smells, the sounds—we know them in our very bones; they're an indelible fixture in our consciousness. But it often happens that we can't translate this intimate knowledge into the conceptual language of a map.[10]

Before the advent of Google Maps, many of us faced a common dilemma when people stopped to ask us for directions in the places we knew the best. We could *take* them to the desired location, but we were powerless to rattle off the necessary street names and distances for them to reach their destination. Another example would be the odd confusion that sets in when I ask my wife to say one of our numerous passwords out loud. We learn very quickly that saying it out loud is not the same as typing it out on a phone or computer, and it often takes a keyboard or a simulated motion to bring the information out into the open air. Paradoxically, there are some things we know too well to articulate. This same dilemma is what was transpiring between my friend and the unsuspecting students. It's not that they don't know what they believe but that they know it too well to put it into words.

Taylor employs the term *social imaginary* to describe this pre-theoretical experience of the circumstances of our lives. It's a very useful way to understand the odd disconnect that takes place when we ask people to translate these experiences into technical terminology. Channeling Augustine, James K. A. Smith argues that "the driving center of human action and behavior is a nexus of loves, longings, and habits that hums along under the hood, so to speak, *without needing to be thought about*."[11] While it's true, for instance, that many college students are default hedonists, precious few of them would describe their spring break exploits with this kind of textbook terminology. As Taylor says, "Humans operated with a social imaginary well before they ever got into the business of theorizing about themselves."[12] We all know that people don't go to Miami Beach to theorize. The notion that unrestricted freedom (much of it physical) is the key to ultimate fulfillment is just something that hums along under millions of people's hoods. Most of them don't even need to use words; they simply confirm the conviction with their bodies.

Of course, these convictions are frequently at odds with reality. We've all had the galling experience of having our cherished misconceptions exposed by reality. We can laugh off the trivial examples involving Santa Claus and the Tooth Fairy, but we move into decidedly more sensitive territory when we read the results of unrestricted freedom on the bathroom scale or when we wake from the stupor of spring break to find ourselves hissing at the conflagration of the morning sun like a scorched vampire. Call to mind those "What You Think You Look Like Versus What You Actually Look Like" memes that dramatize the comic disparity between perception and reality, and you'll have a pretty good picture of our superficial grasp of our place in the world (or the mirror).[13] In theological terms, inhabiting the kingdom of man is second nature to all of us; inhabiting the kingdom of heaven requires fierce devotion and a keen sense of awareness.

Looking back to that kitchen in the Christian household of my adolescence, we might ask, What intimate knowledge precluded a straight answer to my dad? What did I know too well to say out loud? What kingdom did I inhabit? Why *did* I call myself a Christian?

I called myself a Christian because I knew that Christ was real, and I didn't have the luxury of an earnest seeker's doubt. My childhood was circumscribed by what sociologists call "thick religion," a rich constellation of habits and patterns of behavior that exercised an indelible impact on my whole personality and confirmed for me that Christianity was nothing less than a comprehensive way of life. It was in such a setting and such a household that Christ called me to himself when I was five.

From that day forward the whole quality of my existence was permanently altered. The change itself was quite ineffable, and the best I can do to capture some measure of it in words is to say that, though it's possible for me to miss the company of others, I never feel truly alone. A feeling of complete loneliness and isolation has been absent from my life since age five. My world is not haunted or vacant like the deserted cathedrals of my childhood; it's perpetually inhabited. Nothing truly qualifies as wilderness for me. The words of Psalm 139 in this chapter's epigraph are not some kind of inspirational gloss. They accurately convey my lived experience of God's unshakeable presence.

At times the Lord's presence is welcome. A secret joy permeates the rhythms of my day, and I walk around a bit like a person in love. Every song and cloud and sunset is somehow a love letter to me, and Calvin's statement about the world being a theater of God's glory seems like something I need to scream from the rooftops—or at the very least post on social media.

At other times, though, the Lord's presence is downright oppressive, and a deep sense of foreboding characterizes my actions, most of which come down to a form of hiding. Adam and Eve got creative and utilized their surroundings for concealment. Nowadays, we don't even have to leave the couch: We just fall through the trapdoor of our phones to hide from the Lord. In spiritual terms the word *distraction* is nearly always shorthand for hiding. It's why Pascal famously said that most of our problems come down to the fact that we can't sit quietly for an hour in our rooms (try it).[14] It's why the prophet Jonah tried to drown out his Lord's voice by getting on the wrong ship and then sleeping through a catastrophic storm until his panicked shipmates insisted that he get back in touch with reality.

My dad's question opened my eyes to the fact that I was a traitor—that I'd turned my back on the one I knew to be my Lord and Savior. I didn't inhabit some liminal space between belief and unbelief where I could comfortably recline and serve two masters. In truth the day we recognize that we've truly compartmentalized our Christianity is the day we recognize we need to give our lives to Christ. As Austria had already shown me, there's no such thing as nominal Christianity—Christianity reduced to a social club, an empty tradition, or a fashion statement.

That is, a question never arises in a vacuum. It's borne out of a multitude of highly personal circumstances. Behind Dad's question was, of course, a father's concern for the spiritual well-being of his son. However, there was another question hovering in the background, this one from our Lord. As we'll see in chapter seven, the apostle Peter's shortcomings have become a tremendous source of encouragement to me because they poignantly demonstrate God's grace in the midst of our failures. The question behind Dad's question was the same one put to Peter by the resurrected Jesus: "Do you love me?" (John 21:15-17). The question of why I called myself a Christian really amounted to, Do I love Jesus? The next three chapters trace the (often painful) story of how I answered our Lord in the affirmative.

PART THREE

A SON'S RESPONSE TO THE THREE MISCONCEPTIONS

7

FAILING SUCCESSFULLY

Portrait of the Artist as a Young Failure

As it is, I rejoice not because you were grieved,
but because you were grieved into repenting. For you felt
a godly grief, so that you suffered no loss through us.

2 Corinthians 7:9

When Mom knocked on my office door—yes, I also work with my mother—and handed me my old high school transcripts with a wry smile, I braced myself. She'd been doing some spring cleaning and stumbled across the incriminating documents. Retracing my chicken-legged adolescent steps is always a humbling exercise. According to these impassive documents, my sophomore year is particularly unforgiving. Scanning them, I see I'd managed to pass one out of six courses, a drama class, the first day of which began with a corporate rendition of the Hokey Pokey if that tells you anything about its rigors. I still remember dancing Mr. Riesman bellowing, "You put your butt in, you put your butt out and you shake it all about," and thinking, *Well, these participation points are going right out the window*. For the record, the Hokey Pokey is *not* very metal.

Of course, my abysmal academic performance wasn't easy for my folks. It didn't help that several of their friends had raised roving packs of overachievers. We'd hear about their bulging list of fridge-worthy exploits—dean's lists, athletic scholarships, acceptance to competitive universities, ensuing European studies abroad, and prestigious internships—in family newsletters that came replete with gorgeous photos featuring matching spotless shirts. (Guess which kitchen appliance these pristine pictures decorated.)

Meanwhile, my mom and dad were hopeful that I'd somehow manage to graduate on time. Fridge stardom may have waved bye-bye to my freshman year, but there was still hope that I'd walk away from the whole ordeal with a diploma. As it happens I did manage to graduate on time, thanks in no small part to summer school, night classes, some truly creative teachers, not to mention the heroic restraint of my long-suffering mom as she shuttled me around on my grand tour of Georgia's alternative educational institutes. Did I mention I didn't get my driver's license until I was nineteen?

For the sake of brevity, I'll boil my adolescent failures down to a concise list: sports (tried to be the *I* in team), school (all academic aspirations ended the day I got a guitar), girls (maybe it had something to do with the T-shirts filled with bloody chainsaws and pentagrams), driver's test (twice—unbearable self-consciousness), friendship (excused reclusiveness as being European), and Christianity (mistook intellectual assent for devotion to Christ). We'll come back to that last one in a bit.

Parents, was I your worst nightmare? What if I told you that Mom and Dad, far from passively enduring reams of wretched progress reports and teacherly bromides like "he just needs to apply himself," *allowed* me to chart a course that took me far from fridge stardom? What if I told you that they allowed me to fail? And what if I told you that this was the best thing they could've done for me?

PRACTICAL ATHEISM AND
OUR CHRONIC FEAR OF FAILURE

The *New Yorker* once profiled an unusual app. Known as "Days of Life," its application is to tell you how long you have left to live. Feed it your date of birth, gender, and country of residence, and it rewards you with a final countdown of sorts. Mark O'Connell, the author of the piece, offers this vivid distillation, "And, suddenly, you're looking at your life in pie-chart form: a handy infographic of personal transience, an illustration of how close you're getting to being dead. It's the Quantified Self in its most reductive form."[1] Tellingly, this tool is filed under the "productivity" folder of the app store, the idea being that this little mortality alarm will increase your motivation to get stuff done.

Social critics often point to the lamentable modern habit of determining a person's value based on their output. All too often we inhabit a kind of assembly-line mindset that reduces our very existence to "measurable outcomes." Think about a seemingly innocuous phrase like "I've had a very productive day!" Our near-constant reliance on metrics belies an estimation of value that's equal parts mechanistic and reductive. In his book *The Way of the (Modern) World*, Craig M. Gay argues that one of the most insidious byproducts of our modern world is the habit of living as though God does not exist: "Stated bluntly, it is the assumption that even if God exists he is largely irrelevant to the real business of life."[2] A disgruntled customer, a dishonest contractor, a dissatisfied client, a disorganized accountant—if the very idea of prayerfully seeking the Lord's wisdom on dealing with each of these people strikes us as irrelevant and counterproductive, we have reason to pause and reconsider how God's existence reframes the business of life. If he is indeed real, how could we fail to actively seek his will in all of our pursuits?

Most of us are well acquainted with the "Quantified Self in its most reductive form" because of our relentless techniques for measuring success: We measure the days of our lives, our income, our spending, our social media usage, our followers, our friends, our likes, our caloric intake, our exercise, our steps, our heart rates, our sleep patterns. We have personality tests to help us measure our moods, modify our behavior, and monitor our relationships. Speaking of relationships, we have dating apps crafted by relationship "experts" to help us find a "match" that's "compatible" with our particular physique and personality. In many ways our vision of human flourishing amounts to little more than a proliferation of numbers.

Compatibility is a particularly hideous word when it's used in conjunction with human beings. Machines are compatible; human beings are never less than relational. It's roughly the difference between sticking a plug into an electrical outlet and making love. If that sounds crude, consider the fact that sex robots are no longer confined to science fiction and that a good deal of our entertainment is preoccupied with our increasingly romantic relationship with technology.[3]

Reflecting on an ad for lotion that dehumanized its subject by displaying only her torso, Wendell Berry draws attention to "the gravitation of attention from the countenance, especially the eyes, to the specifically sexual anatomy."[4] The fact that the advertising industry routinely dismembers the human body to appeal to our hollow sexual fantasies is revealing. These images offer yet another glimpse of our emaciated understanding of personhood.

With its driving assumption that people are nothing more than objects for self-gratification, pornography in particular is one of the most ruthlessly materialistic institutions operating in the modern world. The fact that so many (Christian and non-Christian alike) are in its thrall demonstrates the practical atheism that's widespread in our culture.[5] In sharp contrast Berry reminds us of the beauty of the Christian vision of sexual union:

The difference, of course, is that the countenance is both physical and spiritual. There is much testimony to this in the poetic tradition and elsewhere. Looking into one another's eyes, lovers recognize their encounter as a meeting not merely of two bodies but two living souls. In one another's eyes, moreover, they see themselves reflected not narcissistically but as singular beings, separate and small, far inferior to the creature that they together make.[6]

Though there's nothing inherently wrong with wearing a Fitbit or setting measurable goals, the habit of viewing humanity in completely instrumental terms has more in common with the primitive behaviorism of B. F. Skinner than it does with Christianity.[7]

Given the prevalence of the assembly-line mindset, it's little wonder that so many young people feel a suffocating sense of urgency when it comes to their future. The counseling services at universities are being stretched well beyond their limits by students who are buckling under the weight of this pressure. Pointing out that these young men and women are "coddled," haven't known true hardship, or simply need to grow up and tighten their resolve largely misses the point. Many of these young people have internalized the notion that they don't deserve to live unless they succeed—that they must justify their own existence. Sadly, parents often reinforce this habit of mind with the best of intentions: "I just want what's best for my kids"; "I have high expectations because I love them"; "I just know that you're capable of so much more"; "If you don't apply yourself, you're going to miss out! Opportunity knocks once!" (Incidentally, this is also why we struggle so mightily to find a place for the unborn, the disabled, and the elderly and infirm. If our functional, on-the-ground view of human value amounts to little more than raw capability, we will on general principle exclude a vast segment of the population, including the most vulnerable members of our society.)

The fear of failure is a perennial human anxiety, of course. But here we see why it's reached epidemic proportions in our cultural moment. If today's default is to measure people's value based on their achievements, success becomes a matter of life and death. We're not just trying to make great SAT scores or get into the right college; we're trying to prove that we deserve to live. Success is cast as personal redemption. Recall the Emerson quote from the introduction: "History is an impertinence and an injury, if it be any thing more than a cheerful apologue or parable of my being and becoming."[8] This poetic rendering of radical autonomy is as bewitching as it is burdensome. Emerson is making clear that the only way to solidify your identity is through your accomplishments in defiance of all the limitations imposed by your circumstances. Why do you think we're so fond of rags-to-riches stories? When the stakes are this high, failure can and will result in despair. Consequently, this is a mindset with numerous casualties. The great tragedy is that it's also based on a conception of human worth that's completely false. It's simply an outworking of practical atheism.

Practical atheism emerges whenever we betray two tacit assumptions: (1) the material world is all that matters, and (2) our salvation is located in human achievement. John Gray, himself a thoroughgoing skeptic, points out that this ambition is simply a repackaging of the Christian salvation narrative, with humanity replacing Christ as the savior.[9] In this sense, many so-called Christian households are filled with practical atheists, well-meaning men and women who believe that worship, prayer, and Scripture are all wholesome, uplifting pursuits that nevertheless have little to no bearing on their day-to-day lives. They leave the church, the Bible study, the prayer meeting, the camp, the conference and go back to the "real world" of finals and competitive internships. Within the world of higher education, the STEM (science, technology, engineering, mathematics) hegemony is yet another outworking of the mindset that construes this world as all that there is and human achievement as our sole means of deliverance.

This line of thinking is far from absent in Christian homes. In their extensive research on teenagers growing up in Christian households, Kara Powell and Steven Argue uncovered a deeply revealing struggle: *busyness*. Many young people experience a dramatic spike in stress and anxiety because of the relentless pace of their lives. Sadly, parents are often oblivious to the pressure they're putting on their kids and continue to fill up the roster in an effort to guarantee future success. "Once a source of love and support, the family has become the vehicle (pun intended) that drives teenagers from one activity to the next."[10] I speak from experience: my wife teaches music, and I'm continually astonished by the schedules of her students. From music lessons to volunteer work to play practice to sports events to meetings with college recruiters, these young people operate at the speed of a CEO. Though the reasons behind this agenda are legitimate enough—gaining admission to college, locking down a summer internship, and so on—the frantic sense of urgency also belies our era's trademark obsession with control and measurable outcomes. The result is that our teenagers feel the (frequently unvoiced) need to justify their existence through their achievements.

Hans Boersma shares a sobering story of the subtle ways practical atheism infiltrates the Christian imagination. On a field trip to the *Body Worlds* exhibit with a Christian high school, Boersma was taken aback by the breezy enthusiasm of his fellow evangelicals for these displays of plasticized human corpses, which showcased our era's ubiquitous objectification and exploitation of the human body. Content to label the exhibition as an example of how we are "fearfully and wonderfully made," these teachers and students didn't recognize that they were unwittingly endorsing the rampant reductionism that underwrites our modern estimation of human value. "Rather, I have become convinced that a certain kind of appeal to the goodness of creation, such as the one I just described, lapses into its opposite: that is, a denigration and commodification of the created order, in this case the human body."[11] Imagine someone telling Wendell Berry that the dismembered female torso from the lotion ad was an example of how we are fearfully and wonderfully made.

Publicly displaying a person's internal organs like slides in a laboratory is not a celebration of creation; it's a sad reflection of the hollow materialism that most of us take for granted. Such commodification often misleads us into thinking that biology (or any other kind of scientific field) exhausts our understanding of personhood. This is the reason why, for many people, scientists (especially surgeons and physicists) function as modern priests. It's also the reason why many of us view prayer as a last resort—the place to which we retreat when medicine and all other modern miracles have proven ineffective.

PUSHING PAST THE FEAR OF FAILURE

But powerful lies remain lies. If Christianity is true, the *quantified self* in all its reductive forms turns out to be a particularly vivid idol of our age. Most importantly, our value is not predicated on our talents and abilities. If it were, countless human beings would no longer matter. Rather, we are endowed with infinite worth by our Lord because we are made in his image. Since this worth is conferred by the Lord, it is irrevocable and extends to every human being, including those on the margins. When we internalize these truths, it's possible not only to experience failure without being crushed but also to learn from our failures and to grow.

In recent years several celebrated academics have reminded us that behind every successful résumé is a long list of failures.

Johannes Haushofer, an assistant professor of psychology and public affairs at no less an institution than Princeton University, is one of the more recent people to publish a "CV of failures." Haushofer believes that many of our unrealistic expectations regarding success persist because of our habit of keeping our failures invisible. His aim in publishing the CV of failures is therefore to "balance the record and provide some perspective."[12] May his tribe increase.

Perhaps our unwillingness to confront our shortcomings is to blame for the deeply misguided belief that we can somehow spare our children from the necessary pains of failure. From the bruises and lacerations on a healthy toddler's legs to the bumper-car dynamics of a budding driver with a learner's permit and a teenager's sense of immortality, we know that failure is an integral part of any form of success. On the one hand, we need to set up rules and boundaries to safeguard our kids and curb self-destructive behavior. On the other hand, we have to acknowledge that they'll never learn unless we allow them (within reason) to make mistakes. We also need to remember that we can't save ourselves, and we certainly can't save our kids. Christians are the ones who have turned to Christ for that very reason.

FAILURE LEADING TO DISCERNMENT

Like aging, sickness, and death, failure is a guarantee. I know that's a bummer of a sentence, but we've all got insider knowledge here, even if we're supposed to drown it in beach trips, margaritas, and binge-worthy shows. Maintaining a constant image of success is an unwritten law of North American social etiquette. Think of the sardonic lines from the real-estate mogul in the 1999 film *American Beauty*: "In order to be successful, one must project an image of success at all times."[13]

This perpetual charade is soul-wearying business. Imagine permanently inhabiting the mindset and comportment of a formal dinner—the kind of function where you chew carefully and assiduously avoid anything messy. (I know I'm not the only one who handles the food on my plate like radioactive material in these strained circumstances—stick with soups if you can.) Given the pervasive nature of online culture, many of us feel like we're at a kind of never-ending business dinner. As the line between public and private becomes more and more blurred, it's hard to avoid the demand to always be "on," the demand to project an image of success at all times.

But despite all of our efforts, failure remains unavoidable. Since it's unavoidable, however, it follows that there are legitimate ways of responding to it—there are ways to fail well. Thus we arrive at the paradoxical notion of successful failure. The fruit of successful failure is discernment. Looking back on my adolescence, I have come to see my parents' decision to allow me to fail as extraordinarily brave and wise. I know they endured their share of sleepless nights, but their hopes for me went well beyond the slick sheen of a fridge-worthy performance; they wanted me to be the kind of person who exhibited true discernment rather than mere proficiency at jumping through a given set of hoops. Sadly, most of us know people who perform well and live poorly. My parents saw my own flourishing in more holistic terms.

Etymologically, the word *discernment* combines two crucial forms of insight, namely, penetration and discrimination. Discerning people are thus able to see into the heart of a given matter while maintaining proper distinctions.[14] In effect, discernment points to something and says "this," and in so doing also offers a crucial distinction by saying "not this."

If this sounds a bit abstract, think about diamonds. To the untrained eye most diamonds look identical apart from size. But as any expert will tell you, each diamond is highly unique, and only the most refined techniques will help to establish its value. Because of diamonds' elaborate geological formation, the Gemological Institute of America (GIA) calls each one a "miracle of time and place," as unique as a snowflake. The GIA is famous for introducing the 4Cs, which form the standard criteria for estimating the value of a diamond. The 4Cs are color, clarity, cut, and carat.[15]

Each of these categories requires scrupulous attention to detail. A diamond achieves its highest color grading when it's colorless or as nearly colorless as possible. This quality is established by comparing the diamond with a master stone. Clarity has to do with a diamond's purity. Given its arduous journey to the earth's surface, diamonds frequently pick up what mineralogists call "inclusions"— a euphemism for flaws. Most of these flaws are not visible to the naked eye, but under 10x magnification they are readily apparent. The highest mark that a diamond can earn concerning clarity is FL, which stands for flawless. The uninitiated may be surprised to hear that a diamond's cut is much more about the transmission of light than it is about the shape. "Diamonds are renowned for their ability to transmit light and sparkle so intensely. We often think of a diamond's cut as shape (round, emerald, pear), but a diamond's cut grade is really about how well a diamond's facets interact with light."[16] A successful cut thus requires a supreme level of artistry and craftsmanship. The fourth *C* is the most straightforward: carat simply refers to the weight of the stone. Taken together, the 4Cs offer a near-panoramic view of discernment, showcasing its deep perception as well as its highly discriminating gaze.

For a fulsome picture of discernment in the world of human affairs, look no further than Christ's response to the widow's offering in Luke's Gospel:

> Jesus looked up and saw the rich putting their gifts into the offering box, and he saw a poor widow put in two small copper coins. And he said, "Truly, I tell you, this poor widow has put in more than all of them. For they all contributed out of their

abundance, but she out of her poverty put in all she had to live on." (Luke 21:1-4)

A surface-level reading of these offerings would simply equate the more substantial gifts with greater generosity. But Christ's gaze is always penetrating, taking us well beyond mere outward appearances. Noting the widow's impoverished circumstances, he draws attention to the fact that she gives "all she had to live on," whereas everyone else is simply drawing from their surplus. Her gift is greater because it demands tremendous self-sacrifice, and personal cost remains one of the greatest litmus tests of a person's actual generosity. Plenty of folks love to be seen as generous. Precious few are willing to pay the high cost of real generosity. By illuminating the selfless motivations behind the widow's gift, Christ distinguishes her from those who are doing little more than fulfilling a social obligation.

Think also of the apostle Paul's famous message to the Athenians in Acts 17. Surveying their wealth of religious iconography, Paul perceives a deep-seated spiritual yearning and points to the altar with the inscription "to the unknown god" as especially emblematic of this yearning (v. 23). Tellingly, he quotes from two pagan poets to underscore the point, calling us God's "offspring" and arguing that "in him we live and move and have our being" (v. 28). But Paul does more than cut to the heart of the matter; he introduces a crucial distinction by invoking Christ and his resurrection, thus exhorting his audience to move beyond the amorphous spirituality of the barren altar. He calls us to serve not an unknown god but *the* living God. Compressed into this marvelous passage is a rich blueprint for all holistic cultural engagement, one that showcases the twin necessities of deep perception and proper discrimination. As Paul demonstrates, we can and must affirm the deep spiritual longings that we encounter in our cultural landscape while also recognizing the proper boundaries of these diverse expressions.

Discernment is interested in the fine details. While Paul acknowledges that the altar showcases legitimate spiritual hunger, he swiftly transports his listeners to a firm destination:

> What therefore you worship as unknown, this I proclaim to you. The God who made the world and everything in it, being Lord of heaven and earth, does not live in temples made by man, nor is he served by human hands, as though he needed anything, since he himself gives to all mankind life and breath and everything. And he made from one man every nation of mankind to live on all the face of the earth, having determined allotted periods and the boundaries of their dwelling place, that they should seek God, and perhaps feel their way toward him and find him. (v. 23-27)

APOCALYPTIC REALISM AND THE REWARDS OF RECOGNIZING FAILURE

Failure can and often does engender discernment, and the painful lesson usually comes courtesy of a collision with boundaries. For the most part, we crash into boundaries when we don't recognize them or try to defy them.

Our musicals may extol the virtues of defying gravity, but most of us learn firsthand that this is a fool's errand. It's the reason our son's pediatrician noted the cuts and bruises on his legs with approval: "That's what I like to see. It means he's *learning*." Learning from falling and failing, that is. Discipline in the early years works in much the same way. When no becomes your child's mantra, a crash course with boundaries has been charted. Through countless tantrums and Band-Aids, these boundaries become firmly established, and the child learns to navigate the physical and moral space of your home and, eventually, the world. Stated in the most elemental terms, what my wife and I want for our children as they grow into maturity is the ability to make wise decisions—to say both "this" and "not this." We want deep insight and discrimination. In a word, we want discernment. We want our kids to transmit the light of Christ like a well-cut diamond, with the full recognition that those jeweler's cuts are rarely painless.

In many ways the teenage years simply reprise the toddler phase with a higher level of sophistication: Your toddler will yell no or melt in your arms, but your teenager will tell you a compelling story as they justify their infractions. Few of us are novelists, but most of us are gifted storytellers when it helps us get what we want.

Since teenagers aren't machines, they don't come with owner's manuals. There's no life hack for mastering an adolescent. Once again, though techniques, strategies, and methodologies all have their place in human affairs, attempting to solve the problem that is your kid has more in common with B. F. Skinner's "social conditioning" projects than it does with Christianity. It's the reason this book doesn't have *Seven Easy Steps to Fixing Your Child* as a subtitle.

I can't offer you seven easy steps to fix your child, but I can draw from the wisdom of my parents when they navigated—endured is more like it—my teenage years.

In *Desiring the Kingdom*, James K. A. Smith argues that the church needs "a contemporary apocalyptic—a language and a genre that sees through the spin and unveils for us the religious and idolatrous character of the contemporary institutions that constitute our own milieu."[17] He doesn't mean that pastors need to try their hand at writing dystopian fiction. To see the world through apocalyptic lenses doesn't yield smoldering visions of decimated cities and roving bands of ragged survivors. Rather, it reveals the spiritual realities behind the curtain. Consider Richard Bauckham's description of the spiritual dynamic of the book of Revelation:

> Revelation provides a set of Christian prophetic counter-
> images which impresses on its readers a different vision of

the world: how it looks from the heaven to which John is caught up in chapter 4. The visual power of the book effects a kind of purging of the Christian imagination, refurbishing it with alternative visions of how the world is and will be.[18]

In this sense, the quantified self is an apocalyptic figure because it discloses the nature of so much contemporary idolatry—namely, our tendency to turn technology and convenience into a graven image. In response to Smith's challenge for a contemporary apocalyptic, I offer the category of *apocalyptic realism*, which is a sensibility that takes its cues from Revelation by recognizing both the impermanence of our world as well as its deep-seated spiritual underpinnings. Like Solomon in Ecclesiastes, like Paul in Athens, like John on the island of Patmos, the apocalyptic realist views the world from an eternal perspective. An apocalyptic realist will marvel at the splendor of the natural world while also noting its transitory nature. Apocalyptic realists know that flowers bloom in both meadows and cemeteries, and that the sun rises gloriously over churches and cancer clinics alike. Apocalyptic realists also recognize that there's no such thing as pure secularity—no neutral, a-religious, nonpartisan sphere where we can pursue the common good with zero ideological interference. The apocalyptic realist agrees with David Foster Wallace that "in the day-to-day trenches of adulthood, there's no such thing as atheism."[19]

We might point to the *Body Worlds* exhibit as a celebration of that fact that we're fearfully and wonderfully made. An apocalyptic realist would reply that this is simply practical atheism in disguise—a viewpoint that's underwritten by scientific naturalism rather than the Lord of all creation. Likewise, if Christian parents push their child to attain a form of success that has more in common with contemporary culture than it does with the biblical vision of salvation, the apocalyptic realist will remind them of Paul's piercing words regarding the obstinacy of unbelievers: For all our talk of Benedict Options and cultural crises, most of us simply operate as though all is well and that the current arrangement is just the way it is.[20] So we resign ourselves. In the words of Walker Percy—an apocalyptic realist par excellence— "Beware of people who think that everything is okay."[21]

Though he didn't use the phrase, my dad helped to foster apocalyptic realism in our household. He taught us to see how human culture looks from heaven, and he did this by subtly parting the curtain and revealing the hidden idols of our age. I remember watching a sitcom as a family and Dad calmly pointing out that it was presenting us with a world devoid of all serious moral consequences. Dishonesty, infidelity, sexual abuse, wanton promiscuity and objectification, vicious gossip, and even murder—all were trivialized and emptied of any true moral significance. As Dad said, in good apocalyptic realist fashion, "This is just socially acceptable nihilism." Believe it or not, these observations arose organically at the moment. Dad wasn't reading from a script or sniffing out a teaching moment, and he certainly wasn't one of those annoying sages who just can't resist demonstrating their spiritual superiority by trashing all of your favorite shows. He *liked* the shows and laughed with us. But he also wanted us to see that Walker Percy is right; everything is *not* okay. My dad helped us distinguish between the kingdom of heaven and Babylon.

Let's return once more to the kitchen on that fateful morning when Dad asked me why I called myself a Christian. Part of the reason the question landed with such force is that Dad had imparted to me an eternal perspective, one that remains irrevocable. Once I saw the world through apocalyptic lenses, I couldn't unsee the vision. Dad's question did more than expose my hypocrisy. It exposed the idols of my heart. Like so many so-called Christians, I offered lip service to the gospel, but the shape of my life betrayed the same practical atheism that surrounded me. I believed that this world was all that mattered, and I believed I could save myself through my achievements. I may have put all my eggs in the death-metal basket instead of an Ivy League education, but my basic aspirations matched all those seeking salvation on human terms.

FAITH BORN OF FAILURE

One of my more devastating failures arrived when I was in my late twenties. In keeping with the highly personal nature of most of our failures, this one runs the risk of appearing trite on the outside. I assure you it was spirit-wrecking. I'd become convinced that I was called to be a writer, and I decided that I needed to study in a formal setting. In good strategic fashion I applied to only one highly competitive program, reasoning that this degree was practically written in the stars. But, as we all know, it's easy to mistake desire for destiny. I was promptly rejected. When I opened the envelope and read the standard "Dear John" verbiage, I thought my life was ending. In bed that night I was surprised to hear myself say out loud, "If I can't be a great writer, I don't want to be." My wife regarded me with sober eyes, "Well, then I think you need to examine your heart."

The next day I did something that nearly made me physically sick. I closed my office door, got down on my knees, and thanked the Lord for the rejection. It was a touchstone moment in my spiritual life because it opened my eyes to the idolatry colonizing my heart. I saw that I was making that most American of mistakes, conflating my identity with my achievements. Before the rejection, if you'd asked me the source of my salvation, I would've told you it was Jesus Christ. I was once again sliding into a habit of mind that replaces the Lord's grace with one's gifting. I was actually trying to save myself. Though I suspect this is a tendency that will remain a thorn in our flesh this side of eternity, it's possible to avoid being crippled by it if we learn the painful lesson of placing our earthly endeavors in their proper context. Being a celebrated writer is, of course, a laudable achievement. But expecting it to repair one's soul amounts to seeking redemption through transitory talents and abilities. A casual glance at people who have "made it" reveals that massive gifting is often a mixed blessing. It's hard to focus on our limitations when our ears are ringing with constant applause. Though I may wince as I say it, I've grown to thank the Lord for not placing this kind of burden on my shoulders.

I will never stop being grateful for the Bible's unflinching depiction of failure. According to Dallas Willard, "It is in Peter and his life that we begin to get a glimpse of what is *really* possible for human life."[22] How hopeful and how revealing that this glimpse comes through such a faulty vehicle—for Peter's spiritual victory has its roots in abject failure.

Willard opens his discussion of the apostle by distinguishing between conversion and the spiritual transformation that follows in the life of a believer. The fact that so many North American Christians don't even recognize the distinction shows just how unrealistic our expectations are concerning spiritual maturity.[23] Without putting it into words, we seem to believe that a conversion experience (especially a dramatic one) will produce a momentum sufficient to bypass all major impediments to spiritual growth. We often think conversion precludes the rest of our lives. In Willard's words, "When we think of 'taking Christ into the workplace' or 'keeping Christ in the home,' we are making our faith into a set of *special* acts. The 'specialness' of such acts just underscores the point—that being a Christian, being Christ's isn't thought of as a normal part of life."[24]

We get saved and quickly return to life as usual. This is the reason many so-called Christian households operate as though God is a distant reality that only has a bearing on their existence on Sundays, holidays, and when they're at a point of crisis or close to death. It's the reason Dad's question about why I called myself a Christian infuriated me. I might as well have responded, "What's that got to do with anything?" For me, at the time the answer was "nothing." What's the answer for you?

In Colossians 1:28, Paul uses paternal language once again as he writes to this young church he has worked so hard to nurture. Calling to mind the "riches of the glory of this mystery" (v. 27) of Christ revealed to the Gentiles, he writes, "Him we proclaim, warning everyone and teaching everyone with all wisdom, that we may present everyone mature in Christ." As we've seen, maturity requires a successful encounter with failure. That is, failure leading to discernment.

My parents weren't content with lip service—they were aiming to present me mature in Christ. That's why Dad ambushed me with that question. If his question brings discouragement to you, think of Peter once again. Bold, headstrong, and adventurous, at times it's difficult to distinguish his courage from his impetuousness. And like so many of us he often starts so well. He's the first out of the boat in the storm, walking on water with his Lord. But soon his eyes are on the turbulent waters and he's sinking like a stone. He's the first to confess Jesus as Lord, but soon his foot is in his mouth when he resists Christ's words concerning his eventual death on the cross. "Blessed are you" followed by "Get behind me, Satan!" (Matthew 16). Quite a mixed track record.

This mixed performance continues on the night of Jesus' betrayal. Though Peter does his level best to defend his rabbi, he receives a swift rebuke when he reaches for his sword and cuts off the right ear of the high priest's servant (John 18:10). Willard points out that Peter initially makes good on his claims to follow his Master, even if it costs him his life. The others fled, but Peter "really was stronger than the others" because he followed at a distance to the palace of the high priest—a bold maneuver given his violent outburst earlier.[25] But despite his good intentions, the night ends in abject failure for Peter, and he fulfills Christ's prophecy by denying him three times before the rooster crows. It's the kind of downfall that could undo anyone. As with the roiling waters on the night that Jesus came to the disciples on the water, Peter took his eyes off his Lord and began to sink. This time he sank to his lowest point. Though he earnestly desired to follow Jesus, the deeply ingrained ways of the flesh catapulted him back into the throes of practical atheism, where the exigencies of his immediate circumstances eclipsed his devotion to his Lord. As Willard puts it, "What a firsthand knowledge Peter gained this night of 'the motions of sins, which work in our members to bring forth fruit unto death' (Rom. 7:5)!"[26]

But Willard is right: Peter truly does show us just how much is possible in human life, even one as tangled, confused, and conflicted as our own. In the end Peter's failures, profound as they are, do not define him. Look no further than the moving scene in John 21:15-17. Instead of a confrontation, Jesus offers a gentle chastisement, asking Peter, "Do you love me?" three times, a number that matches each of his denials. Peter's first two responses are more subdued; his experiences have chastened his tongue. But the final question provokes grief, "Lord, you know everything; you know that I love you" (v. 17). Then Jesus instructs his servant to "feed my lambs," a command that reinstates Peter's ministry and reinforces the prophecy of Matthew 16:18: "And I tell you, you are Peter, and on this rock I will build my church, and the gates of hell shall not prevail against it."

In the end Peter's failures don't prevail against him either. He continued to struggle on occasion (see in Galatians 2:11-13). But his devotion to his Lord remained steadfast, even to the point of death (John 21:18-19). Speaking as someone with numerous failures to my name, I'm greatly encouraged that Scripture numbers

Peter among its heroes. If Peter can be restored, so can you and I, and so can our children. What if our homes reflected this liberating truth? While my parents didn't encourage my failures, they also recognized that they didn't have to define me. In truth, our Maker is the only one with the right to define us. The sooner we recognize that, the better our lives will be.

Failures are inevitable for fallen human beings, but thanks to the exceeding mercy of our Lord they can also serve as key ingredients in our spiritual maturity.

8

LOVING VIRTUOUSLY

We love because he first loved us.

1 JOHN 4:19

hy did I drift into the philosophy section of a now-defunct bookstore chain?

I had zero intellectual aspirations at the time and no intention of ever going to college. I'd graduated high school by the skin of my teeth and was trying to rebrand my chronic loafing as "taking some time to think about my future." But with no clear parameters or set goals, this little interval didn't even rise to the dignity of a gap year. Truth be told, I simply wanted to inhabit that hazy in-between space for an indefinite period, to click pause so that I was perpetually poised between childhood and adulthood. A buoyant lack of responsibilities augmented by the privileges of adulthood—sip a beer, surf the web, but don't worry about paying for the internet. Best of both worlds. My token measure of responsibility was a job at a video store—those beautiful cultural relics. I got five free rentals a week and that was a pretty sweet gig as far as I was concerned. My life was one big daydream.

But drift I did, and the lack of any immediate precedent didn't stop a golden spine from commanding my attention from the bookstore's inert shelves. I squinted and *The Basic Writings of Existentialism* came into focus, neatly piercing my indolence. I had no idea what existentialism was, but it sounded weighty enough to keep me from drifting any further. Those five free rentals would have to wait.

I got home and pored over my discovery. The anthology began with an excerpt from *Fear and Trembling*, Kierkegaard's baroque meditation on Abraham and Isaac's agonized trek up Mount Moriah. The excerpt was titled "Is There a Teleological Suspension of the Ethical?" Up to that point I'd never known that there was a distinct category with a flag marked "ethical." Nor did I imagine that this strange terrain could be *suspended*, let alone in a *teleological* fashion! In all honesty, I had no idea what a *teleology* was. I panicked and called my dad, who was on the road doing apologetics and probably using the word *teleology* every other sentence.

I could hear his smile through the receiver as he began to patiently walk me through the foreign language of "Continental philosophy." This was a moment he'd anticipated for quite a while, and a submerged memory rose like mist from the troubled waters of my mind: Dad staring into my eyes and declaring, "You've got a deep sense of curiosity, son. One day the dam will burst and on that day I'll be ready." At the time this cryptic statement simply left me bewildered. Now it was starting to make sense. Given the current state of my mental life, it was a kind of backhanded compliment: Dad had clocked the torrent of nascent (read, wildly immature) thoughts building up in my skull, and he knew that a breach situation would necessitate a treatment process not unlike water purification.

I plowed ahead in the *Basic Writings*, understanding a fraction of what I read and growing more and more captivated with each page. Far from frustrating, my ignorance was a goad to deeper investigation. The more I read, the bigger the world became. Kierkegaard made me feel like I'd never really read my Bible. Why had I never even considered the psychological torment of Abraham as he went about the painstaking and lengthy preparations to spill his own son's blood? And what about the spiritual upheaval of the fact that the living God—the sum and standard of all goodness—issued this seemingly immoral command? Despite the laconic pace of the biblical narrative, read between the lines and you quickly notice that this beleaguered dad had ample time to think about what he was doing during that long ascent. But, like a good cultural Christian sleepwalking my way through God's Word, I'd spared my brow many a furrow by simply skipping ahead to the providential ram caught in the bushes, and I was more than willing to follow this same ram to the cross if any stray misgivings about the holiness of God cropped up.[1] *Fear and Trembling* is a book-length refusal to cave to that false consolation, and as such it's the book that restored Scripture's hard edges for me.

At the same time I was gaining a vocabulary for describing realities I had long sensed on an intuitive level. The first excerpt that got through and continued to rise like dough in the oven of my mind came from Kierkegaard's *Despair Is the Sickness unto Death*. In his characteristically recondite way, Kierkegaard offers an anatomy of modern despair, construing it as an invisible sickness that colonizes the heart, where it remains undetected as we go about the business of our daily lives. For Kierkegaard despair is at its most severe when it evades our awareness. Plenty of folks who lead what appear to be happy and well-balanced lives, filled with big houses, hypoallergenic dogs, emerald-green lawns, yoga studios, and beautiful towheaded children, are actually experiencing despair in disguise. They're not happy, but they think they are. However, it's not just that they want to convince everyone else of their bliss. Worse, they've fallen under their own spell, and their velvety circumstances only serve to reinforce this counterfeit sense of well-being. With his incisive portrait of the opulence of contemporary despair, Kierkegaard gave me the skeleton key to all those free rentals that chronicled suburban anomie (hello, *Ice Storm*), rabid consumerism (*American Psycho*), and "God's lonely man" in the overcrowded city (*Taxi Driver*).

Naturally, it was only a matter of time before I applied Kierkegaard's haunting insight into my own life. I looked in the mirror and saw through my idle rendition of despair. Years later I discovered that Walker Percy had beat me to the punch with his novel *The Moviegoer*. Designed to be a fictional counterpart to Kierkegaard's book, the story opens with an epigraph from *Despair Is the Sickness unto Death*: "The specific character of despair is precisely this: it is unaware of being despair."[2] *The Moviegoer* introduces us to Binx Bolling, a man who is suddenly aroused from the slumber of his everydayness and begins to approach the mystery of his despairing existence like a detective following clues. Underscoring the everydayness of his despair, the first of these clues arrives via an inventory of the possessions on his bureau:

> I stood in the center of the room and gazed at the little pile, sighting through a hole made by thumb and forefinger. What was unfamiliar about them was that I could see them. A man can look at this little pile on his bureau for thirty years and never once see it. It is as invisible as his own hand. Once I saw it, however, the search became possible.[3]

"The search" is Bolling's general designation for what happens once we've been liberated from the stupor of our everydayness. It's what happens to Plato's prisoner who flees the cave's bewitching shadows, or, to draw from a modern spin on the parable, Neo when he takes the red pill and flees the consoling simulation of the Matrix.[4] Bolling relentlessly exposes our many attempts at finding some kind of superficial relief or premature closure as nothing more than cushy evasions that play right into the hands of despair. Part of the novel's brilliance is the fact that it doesn't pander to our appetite for the exotic and exploitative. Binx doesn't start manu-facturing meth or go on a killing spree—those are the subjects of our entertainment, the premier escape hatch of middle-class de-spair. No, Binx's evasions are of a decisively more domestic and even pedestrian variety: movies, cars, money, women.

For all its inherent risk and subsequent damage, there's a so-bering aspect to extreme behavior because it often blows despair's cover, exposing our true condition. When people in crisis coun-seling circles extol the virtues of hitting rock bottom, this is the kind of wake-up call they have in mind. It's hard to hold on to your illusions of control, for instance, if you're sitting in a haphazard circle of folding chairs in a high school gym and introducing yourself as a fellow addict. This is why the novelist David Foster Wallace uses a halfway house to craft one of the more radiant explorations of spirituality in recent fiction. Despair is poorly hidden in a crisis. Cloak it in the pristine linens and matching curtains of a fine suburban home, however, and you've got an immaculate costume.

Because it reveals our true condition, the search inverts our normal categories so that "what are generally considered to be the best of times" are in fact "the worst of times" and vice versa.[5] Why? If the distinctly modern guise of despair involves a heavy dose of deception, "good times" frequently prove to be its most fertile ground. The laundry list of addictions plaguing our nation is a clear indication of this point. How many times are we led into bondage with the promise of a good time? For an example, look no further than the porn industry, which remains a colossal player in America's economy. By commodifying one of the most sacred expressions of human intimacy, pornography neatly caters to the modern fantasy that happiness simply equates to feeling good. If you think despair and feeling good are incompatible, consider the plight of any addict relishing a fix in the wreckage of her own life and you'll see that we're perfectly capable of feeling good amid desperate misery.

But how are we fooled into thinking that we're happy when we're miserable? The only way to disguise subjective satisfaction as happiness is to avoid all true self-awareness. Our culture may epitomize narcissism and self-aggrandizement, but it does so through an increasingly exaggerated lens that insulates us from honest introspection. In short, selfies generally don't promote true self-awareness; their carefully manicured images have more in common with a funhouse mirror than with honest portraits. If you don't believe me, try on a bathing suit in the unforgiving light of a dressing room, and you'll quickly see the difference.

So many of our "good times" depend on a fundamental lack of self-awareness. The real ingenuity of pornography consists in its ability to distract us from the fact that we're indulging in it. Indeed, any level of self-awareness is lethal to the enterprise. Its machinery is designed to trick us into thinking that we're much more than a leering spectator. If we suddenly lock eyes with our reflection as we're going about this degrading business, the spell is broken. Likewise, the illusion collapses if we're suddenly bombarded with facts that betray the humanity of the people we're objectifying. Imagine a porn video that featured pictures of the stars as babies or interviews where they talked about how their favorite meal was meatloaf and that they hoped to one day open a coffee shop in Brooklyn.

But there's an oddly consoling aspect to our catalog of conspicuous addictions. Since we're comfortable filing porn and substance abuse away as destructive habits, they tend to shine a glaring spotlight on the actual condition of our hearts, and, as grueling as the prospect of facing our moral failings may sound, what Kierkegaard and Binx have in mind is a whole lot more unsettling and insidious. If we want to discover modern despair, we have to look at the places between the crises. We need to look at the times before our cover is blown. We have to follow the inverse logic of Binx's search and look for despair in the "good times" because that's where it hides. When we think that everything in our life is going well, when we think that everything is under control, when we make the fatal mistake of forgetting our total dependence on God—what Scripture refers to as the "fear of the Lord"—we are in profound despair, no matter how resplendent our lives may look.

On the road I'm often asked about how we reach those who are happily living apart from Christ—the so-called happy pagans. I used to think this was a daunting question; now I think it's little more than a misnomer. Despite appearances, true happiness is impossible apart from Christ. If he is indeed your Maker—the one who knit you in your mother's womb and the one who knows you better than you know yourself—how could it be otherwise? Despair has a beguiling wardrobe that includes everything from worldly prosperity to fame and widespread influence, making it all but invisible to those without spiritual discernment. Those who see the world from the standpoint of eternity, however, know that its leathery wings often beat above glittering kingdoms.

RECOVERING SINNERS

Dallas Willard argues that if churches abandoned the consumer Christianity of our day and applied the Twelve Steps of Alcoholics Anonymous (AA) more broadly, we would see a moral revolution.[6] But what does an addiction-recovery program have to do with the life of the church? We can begin to make sense of Willard's proposal by considering the first three steps, which require respectively an admission of our powerlessness in the face of addiction, the recognition of "a power greater than ourselves," and the subsequent surrender of our "will and lives" to this power.[7] In lectures and conversations Willard never tired of insisting that Christians ought to introduce themselves as "recovering sinners," dispensing with the armor of social niceties. It's a wise proposal: "Nice" people are always "doing well," generating glowing newsletters, returning from the perfect vacation with the perfect tan, and maintaining the ideal work-life balance. Recovering sinners, like recovering addicts, take it one day at a time.

Willard is far from alone in pointing to the spiritual power of AA. Over the years several shrewd writers have highlighted the confounding effectiveness of this homely little program. One of the more memorable voices in recent years belongs to a contemporary novelist with a reputation for trafficking in postmodern tropes and making colossal demands of his readers. Boasting 1,079 pages, an immensely convoluted plot that defies neat summary, protean sentences that often span paragraphs and even pages, as well as sprawling endnotes that take up nearly a hundred pages in and of themselves, the late David Foster Wallace's novel *Infinite Jest* seems an unlikely place to encounter a vision that challenges our modern despair. Nevertheless, Wallace uses this towering edifice to rejuvenate our spiritual imagination. By offering a searing account of the triumph of faith in the desolation of our modern addictions, *Infinite Jest* shows us what full-bodied Christian love looks like.

Wallace joins Percy in examining the contours of modern despair, and he's particularly interested in the ambient sadness surrounding our current American landscape. Specifically, why is a place *this* convenient, *this* connected, and *this* affluent so undeniably sad? In an interview with *Salon*, Wallace tries to describe the ineffable sense of unhappiness that dogs our nation:

> There's something particularly sad about [life in America], something that doesn't have very much to do with physical circumstances, or the economy, or any of the stuff that gets talked about in the news. It's more like a stomach-level

sadness. I see it in myself and my friends in different ways. It manifests itself as a kind of lostness.[8]

Infinite Jest chronicles this lostness through the lens of addiction. It's a canny maneuver because a nation that fetishizes feeling good all the time is a nation in which our desires are bound to run amok. Acute despair may slip under the radar, but our numerous addictions paint a picture of increasing lostness on a national scale. While Wallace's book features a near-encyclopedic depiction of substance abuse, his eccentric characters keep reminding us of the spiritual nature of *anything* that captures our hearts. "Our attachments are our temple, what we worship, no? What we give ourselves to, what we invest with faith?"[9] That our "temples" can include everything from a cherished pet to pornography to athletic prowess to opioids is a profound insight that we can trace back to Augustine of Hippo.[10] For Wallace, our various addictions are more than mere distractions and modes of self-gratification; they constitute nothing less than a "distorted religious impulse," and the only way forward is to reorder our worship and learn to love virtuously.[11] Remarkably, this is a clear echo of Augustine's fastidious account of properly ordered loves.[12] In the broken English of one of Wallace's characters, "You are what you love. No? You are, completely and only, what you would die for without, as you say, the *thinking twice*."[13]

Infinite Jest is a work of apocalyptic realism that unveils the inherently spiritual nature of all of our desires and aspirations, whether they show up in an actual temple or not. It unfolds as a kind of spiritual pilgrimage that mirrors Augustine's "road of the affections"—his phrase for capturing the rich tapestry of signs we encounter on our journey to our "true homeland" in the heavenly city.[14] For Augustine these signs took the shape of actual graven images and sacred monuments. For us they show up in ads, memes, movies, music, and shows. Though we're accustomed to seeing Augustine's "road of the affections" in the classic imagery on display in Dante's *Divine Comedy* or Bunyan's *Pilgrim's Progress*, *Infinite Jest* gives us a contemporary road of the affections, one that unfolds in a world where the calendar is now subsidized and the majority of our religious pursuits are invested in the world of entertainment. If Bunyan's Christian must battle dragons and ogres and resist the enticements of Vanity Fair, the characters in *Infinite Jest* must resist the temptations of Demerol and "lethally compelling" movies. Far from a clever gimmick, Wallace sees all these pop culture references as an accurate reflection of our modern scenery: "What I mean by it," he said, "is nothing different than what other people mean in writing about trees and parks and having to walk to the river to get water 100 years ago. It's just the texture of the world I live in."[15] People once took annual pilgrimages to temples and cathedrals. Now they flock to Disneyland.

But if modern despair hides in the good times, and our constellation of distractions only reinforces our false security, how do we wake up? How do we learn to love virtuously amid such abundance? These are matters of life and death because the final destination of misdirected love is bondage. In the words of one of the novel's many recovering addicts, "By the end I was undead, not alive, and I tell you the idea of dyin was nothing compared to the idea of livin like that for another five or ten years and then dyin."[16] The nod to zombies is interesting because *Infinite Jest* hit shelves in 1996, a good while before our current infatuation with all things undead. Tying zombie imagery to addiction is highly perceptive. After all, zombies are the embodiment of mindless consumption. These slobbering ghouls are slaves to their appetites, led willy-nilly on the leash of their urges. In our era of rampant consumerism and ensuing addiction, it's hard not to see them as our decaying doppelgangers.

But Wallace adds a sardonic twist to the Augustinian insight regarding misdirected loves by riffing on Neil Postman's unforgettable title *Amusing Ourselves to Death*. Yes, the phrase "infinite jest" is lifted from *Hamlet*, but it's also the title of a "lethally compelling" piece of entertainment that's circulating in the world of the novel, one that an eager terrorist organization sees as the ideal weapon for subduing a nation enslaved to its desires. It's hard to imagine a more effective weapon in the contemporary United States. The film offers a kind of time-lapse photography of the fate of an impenitent addict. To see it is to become engrossed beyond recovery—newly infantilized viewers slowly starve themselves to death and perish in a mess of their own waste, idiotic grins frozen on their emaciated faces. In a world where numerous people continue to die in pursuit of the perfect selfie, is Wallace's lethal entertainment so far-fetched?

In the words of our Lord, "Truly, truly I say to you, everyone who practices sin is a slave to sin" (John 8:34). This is also Wallace's picture in *Infinite Jest*, and it's the reason that the heart of the book concerns an alcohol-and-drug recovery house, known as Ennet. Wallace deliberately chose to explore the subject of virtuous love in the world of recovery because it's one of the few remaining institutions in post-Christian America where honest introspection is unavoidable:

> The thing is, it has to be the truth to really go over, here. It can't be a calculated crowd-pleaser, and it has to be the truth unslanted, unfortified. And maximally unironic. An ironist in a Boston AA meeting is a witch in church. Irony-free zone. Same with sly disingenuous manipulative pseudo-sincerity. Sincerity with an ulterior motive is something these tough, ravaged people know and fear, all of them trained to remember the coyly sincere, ironic, self-presenting fortifications they'd

had to construct in order to carry on Out There, under the ceaseless neon-bottle.[17]

There's an uneasy parallel between these AA meetings and the testimony circuit in the world of ministry. As I argued earlier, it's easy to hide behind an exotic testimony. In her memoir of addiction and recovery, Leslie Jamison points out that an effective storyteller is often a liability in recovery programs. She highlights one man in particular who finally conceded, "My story isn't much different from anyone's. It's the story of a man who was made a fool of by alcohol, over and over, year after year after year, until finally the day came when I learned that I cannot handle this alone."[18]

Substitute the word *sin* for *alcohol* and that's all of us. Though some people have been delivered from extreme circumstances, at a fundamental level every one of us is in the same boat. We're all sinners in desperate need of God's grace. We're not all former Satanists, drug addicts, and criminals, but every one of us needs to be saved, even—or maybe especially—if we make our home in a sleepy suburban neighborhood. In Wallace's unsparing words, "You are not unique, they'll say: this initial hopelessness unites every soul in this broad cold salad-bar'd hall."[19]

There are no special testimonies, if by *special* we mean that they lay claim to a higher degree of vitality and authenticity. Extreme circumstances do not enhance a person's spiritual credentials. We're all in extreme circumstances. From the discreet gossip of homeowner associations to infidelity to murder, sin is always lethal. We all need to be saved, and, according to Wallace and Willard, we need to stop pretending that we've got it all together, and we're somehow special. If we're Christians, we're recovering sin addicts, learning day by day what it means to crucify "the flesh with its passions and desires" (Galatians 5:24). This is painstaking, unglamorous, "maximally unironic" work, and we take it one day at a time, fiercely guarding against the temptation to think that we're now out of the woods for good. In the words of the late Father Thomas Hopko, "Expect to be fiercely tempted to your last breath."[20] Recovering addicts worldwide would add a hearty amen to that admonition, and Christians ought to as well.

WORTHY TO SEE GOD'S GLORY

Like many kids growing up in Christian households, I hated being dragged to church on Sunday mornings. Now that I'm a dad, I get to inflict the same ordeal on my kids, and I probably enjoy it a little too much. Full circle, as they say.

Not all of us go to AA meetings, but all of us who follow Christ have to go to church, a prospect that often carries the same appeal as an addiction recovery program. The coffee's usually just as bad and the conversations can be just as stilted. I remember sitting down in my small group and cringing as our fearless leader flashed a sappy smile and explained that we were going to "do life together." Along with Wallace, I wondered, *Is this "goofy slapdash anarchic system of low-rent gatherings and corny slogans and saccharine grins and hideous coffee" really the spiritual end of the line this side of eternity?*[21] Wallace levels this same scrutiny at AA through his characters. Much to their chagrin, they discover that, like church, "the thing actually does seem to work."[22] But why does something as aggressively boring, unfashionable, and countercultural as church actually work?

It works because we have to hear and do it over and over again to get it through our thick skulls. And so we drag our weary selves to church on Sunday morning and sing about the gospel for the umpteenth time, recite the creed again, confess the same tired laundry list of sins we never seem to shake, hear yet another leaden sermon, and slink from our pews and shuffle forward like an awkward procession of penguins to take Communion. And somehow it's precisely what we need. We will never reach a point where we've worshiped enough, prayed enough, confessed enough, heard the gospel enough, taken Christ enough.

In truth the problem isn't that church is boring; it's that we don't have our heads on straight. Fickle and finite, it is we who are out of touch with reality, not Christ's church. While we pine for the fading signs of our times, the church offers only the timeless and the eternal. It turns out that church requires a level of refinement that can only be cultivated through spiritual maturity. As C. S. Lewis said so well, it's not that God finds "our desires [...] too strong, but too weak," and church is an invitation to bite off colossally more than we can chew.[23] The great irony is that church routinely disappoints us not because it fails to meet our expectations, but because it exceeds them. As we age, we come to recognize that we don't grow out of church; we can only grow into it.

Speaking of restless kids counting down the minutes in a seemingly endless church service, James K. A. Smith offers a glorious picture of the dawning recognition of what church actually is. He asks us to imagine Andrew, a young boy using his church bulletin as a "checklist" until freedom:

> Confession? Check. Assurance of pardon? Check. Reading of the law? Check. Creed? Check. Pastoral prayer and prayers of the people? Long wait to be able to check that off, as an elder seems to be praying for the entire world. Bible reading? Check. Sermon? Wait for it . . . wait for it . . . still waiting . . . Finally: check! We're getting close! Offering? Check! Wait—second offering for benevolence? Ugh, check (finally). Doxology (we're getting tantalizingly close now): check! Another prayer: check! Andrew can now taste it. A hymn (seven verses!?): finally, check. Here we are, the finish line, T minus thirty

seconds, everyone stands, the end of worship is in sight. Benediction: yes! Freedom![24]

In Smith's illustration, Andrew grows up to relive this same restlessness as he watches his young daughter fidgeting in the pew. He remembers fondly being at that stage when the service felt like an interminable series of hurdles. He sees it differently now, not because he's been assimilated into the lifeless routines of adulthood but because his perspective has been enlarged. You might say his vision has become apocalyptic. Instead of seeing the church service as a monotonous checklist, he now sees it as a great cosmic dance, one that reveals the mystery that "in Christ God was reconciling the world to himself, not counting their trespasses against them, and entrusting to us the message of reconciliation" (2 Corinthians 5:19). Though we make our way through a cultural landscape punctuated by all manner of spiritual longings, God's particular message of reconciliation is made visible in Christ's body alone. But you have to grow up to see it.

One of the more haunting pictures of the church's beauty comes to us in Paul Bunyan's spiritual classic, *The Pilgrim's Progress*. Though we may think of our Sunday morning trek as little more than a tedious obligation, Bunyan speaks of a stately palace called "Beautiful," set by the dangerous "highway side," and "built [by the Lord] for the relief and security of pilgrims."[25] Here, Bunyan's hero, Christian, is refreshed with worship, Communion, and rest. Awakening in the upper chamber known as "Peace," he sings,

Where am I now? Is this the love and care?
Of Jesus, for the men that pilgrims are,
Thus to provide that I should be forgiven,
And dwell already the next door to heaven?[26]

At the end of his time in Palace Beautiful, Christian is led to the top of the house, where he catches a glimpse of the "Delectable

Mountains" of "Immanuel's Land," a foretaste of heaven for his weary eyes.[27] According to Bunyan, this sight is "visible only from within the fellowship of the church."[28]

Not only do we not grow out of church, but as our spiritual vision is deepened, we begin to catch glimpses from it of the other world we were made for. It's in this sense that church is our only true home this side of eternity, the Beautiful Palace standing amid our restless world. It's the one place where we "dwell already the next door to heaven." If we think it's boring, it's because we are far too easily amused.

But where can we turn for a compelling vision of spiritual maturity? Lord knows, there's no end of boring ones available! For many of us, the word *maturity* itself carries joyless connotations of dead-eyed lectures about character formation and the importance of taking responsibility—the kind of things you find in work retreats and finance seminars. Who can show us—Americans spellbound by youth—how exciting growing up is? It's at this juncture that Dante Alighieri emerges as the titan of spiritual maturity among poets—the poet to show us why every Christian can't wait to grow up. *The Divine Comedy* chronicles this poet's long and difficult journey to heaven. The picture we get is one of gradual ascent; Dante begins in hell, moves on to purgatory, and *finally* reaches heaven.[29]

In the poem's final moments we are treated to one of the most profound invitations to spiritual purity and divine communion in all of Western literature. When Dante finally gazes upon Jesus Christ, the "Sum of Grace," his vision is deepened so fantastically that he is "ever more fervent to see in the act of *seeing*."[30] Here the heavenly vision plumbs such unfathomable depths that Dante is powerless to describe it as anything less than an "abyss of light."[31] This "abyss of light" is the ultimate refiner's fire, burning away any last vestige of the old self that would hinder Dante from coming face to face with his Maker. Paul's dark glass has been finally shattered.

C. S. Lewis contends that every earthly desire cloaks a powerful wish "to please God . . . to be a real ingredient in the divine happiness . . . to be loved by God, not merely pitied, but delighted in as an artist delights in his work or a father in a son."[32] Whenever our desires misfire, we discover an eternal appetite in our hearts, and though this experience is never less than painful, it is instrumental in awakening us to the kind of longing that, properly expressed, will lead us straight to the source of our fervent spiritual yearning. Each one of us has beating within our chests an instrument of infinite capacities fashioned by a God of infinite capacities. Because of this, there is a unique fit between our Creator and us. Our urgent need to be known and loved by God is what Lewis aptly calls the "inconsolable secret" of our hearts.[33]

Gazing into the inexhaustible riches of the Living Radiance that is God, Dante finds himself growing in direct proportion to how much of God he is able to see and understand. To his great surprise, the only one who changes amid this progressive revelation is he,

> and not because that Living Radiance bore
> more than one semblance, for It is unchanging
> and is forever as it was before;
> rather, *as I grew worthier to see*, the more I looked,
>   *the more unchanging semblance*
> *appeared to change with every change in me.*[34]

In this moment of supreme adoration, God's vastness finds new expression in Dante's heart. The more of God he has, the more of God he is capable of receiving. But this is an everlasting transaction because the infinite heart Christ has knit within each of us will be satisfied by nothing less than eternity with him. "Blessed are the pure in heart for they shall see God," writes Matthew, and we would do well to remember this verse every time we are tempted to stray into the territory of aimless discipline and vain legalism. Let us never forget that our efforts toward purity and spiritual transformation have a colossal target: We want to see God "as he is. And everyone who thus hopes in him purifies himself as he is pure" (1 John 3:2-3).

Lewis faithfully adapts the spirit of Dante's vision for his Chronicles of Narnia. When Lucy—the most spiritually alert among the children of the Narnia series—is reunited with the great lion, Aslan (the Christ figure of the series), we are treated to this remarkable exchange:

"Aslan," said Lucy, "you're bigger."

"That is because you are older, little one," answered he.

"Not because you are?"

"I am not. But every year you grow, you will find me bigger."[35]

The more we grow in our pursuit of Christ and the riches of his glories, the greater we will find him to be. My prayer for all of us is that when we pause on the threshold of heaven, we will indeed be worthy to see our Maker. On that day, I pray that our wildest dreams will come true, that King Jesus will smile upon us and say, "Well done, good and faithful servant" (Matthew 25:23).

9

IMITATING RIGHTEOUSLY

*Therefore be imitators of God, as beloved children. And
walk in love, as Christ loved us and gave himself up
for us, a fragrant offering and sacrifice to God.*

EPHESIANS 5:1-2

It started with teachers. And it also started innocently enough. Initially, I had no intention of making the impersonations front and center; they were simply a factor in a faithful retelling of a story or anecdote. Take, for instance, one former principal who carefully overenunciated every word and spoke with a Sean Connery lisp (we middle-schoolers waited with bated breath for him to tell us to *sit*). I recall the student body enduring a lengthy disquisition on the moral pitfalls of chewing gum in class, in which he managed to stretch the word *gum* into a languorous moan of doubt: *guuuuum*. I faithfully reproduced this monologue for my mom when she asked me about my day, and to my surprise she laughed. A lot.

Once I realized that this talent could be exploited for the amusement of others, no one was safe. I developed a reliable roster of impersonations that could be deployed at will; I took requests— I still do sometimes, so be careful. Friends asked me if I practiced in front of a mirror, but the truth is that the process is a lot more organic, and it often begins with admiration and affection. Though some of my increasingly exaggerated renditions could verge on cruelty, I *liked* the way my principal talked, and I relished his idiosyncratic speeches. I wasn't actively trying to plunder his mannerisms for amusement and profit. I simply wanted to convey a measure of his distinct personality.

Then there were the impersonations that moved to earnest imitations—the cases where my admiration was so strong that I sought to emulate someone else's personality. We rack up a pretty sizeable roster of these characters over the years. Plenty of them are celebrities, but occasionally one of these mythic creatures steps right into the awkward circumstances of our lives. For me, one of the more memorable cases took place in middle school. This was the year immediately preceding our move from Austria to the United States, and it involved a boy two grades ahead of me. We'll call him Rich.

Rich called himself a punk, and he'd leave his signature—"Punk's Not Dead" (the *a* was always an anarchy sign)—all over our school, and all over Vienna. He smoked prodigiously and swore fluently. He was also a pretty decent skateboarder and occasionally sauntered into class with both a black eye and hickeys on his neck like he'd been necking with a vampire. There were many rumors: he did drugs; he got kicked out of his house; he was wanted by the police; he was close to getting expelled. Whether all this was true is anyone's guess, but there was undeniably dangerous energy about him. The only thing that seemed to make Rich laugh or smile was destruction, whether vandalism or simple damage to school property. I remember him purloining a crude sculpture from art class—the work of some aspiring artist with more sincerity than skill—and chucking it out the fourth-story window into the crowd exiting a grocery store. At the time our school occupied the top floor of a large building in the city. Fortunately, no one was hurt, but an elderly lady did get quite a scare when the sculpture unceremoniously shattered in her grocery cart, apropos of nothing.

I realize this is hardly a charming portrait, but I was spellbound by the kid. He seemed to be from another world—one in which the traditional rules and boundaries didn't apply. Though he usually showed up to school, you got the distinct impression he'd bail as soon as something more amusing caught his attention.

I wanted to be Rich, so I went all out in the impersonations department. I walked like him, talked like him, and dressed like him. Once I even bought his pants. That's right! I paid money for Rich's trousers. They were unwashed and smelled of cigarettes and skater's sweat. Does it get any more authentic? I tried my hand at smoking, too, but quickly abandoned it when I realized that eliminating the incriminating odor required a level of deceptive ingenuity I simply didn't possess. I also started calling myself a punk and scrawling Rich's mantra into school furniture, on train station walls, and on my notebooks and backpack. It was even on the front of my journal. When he caught a glimpse of this, Rich let me know in very unsparing terms that, unfortunately, journals just aren't very punk.

In case that journal didn't give it away, I was *nothing* like Rich. His clothes looked ridiculous on me, his words sounded hollow in my mouth, and his cigarettes were meant for stronger lungs than mine. Unlike Rich, I had a stable home, I'd never been in a serious fight, and I couldn't skate to save my life. Sure, I could pop a Dead Kennedys' tape into my Walkman, but you can't buy true street cred, even when it stoops to sell you a dirty pair of pants.

In the end I couldn't take the impression to its full realization, which would've ended with me closing the gap between my costume and personality. What stopped me was more than my mom's tears and my dad's patient words of admonition—I remember him reading me the full definition of *punk* from the *Oxford English Dictionary* as I winced on our living room couch. Rather, I recognized that Rich's persona had a limited shelf life and that Mom and Dad, for all their missionary getup, Oxford dictionaries, and churchy talk, were offering me something that wouldn't burn away like chaff in the fires of time.

Imitation is a test of character. If the character in question is insubstantial and superficial, the imitation is easily discarded. If the character is robust and full of life, the imitation has something precious: durability. Even at my young age, I could see the fragile nature of Rich's coolness, that his punk persona, though difficult to achieve, was all-too-easily punctured and deflated. Witness the multitude of former punks (or any other former citizens of a sub-culture) who traded in their leather jackets and liberty spikes for venti lattes and cubicles at ad agencies. In sharp contrast, my mom and dad knew "the secret of facing plenty and hunger, abundance and need" (Philippians 4:12). This secret had sustained them as they went about their lonely ministry work in a strange country, and it had sustained them when they were briefly imprisoned for their faith.

From the drive for personal fulfillment to the realm of politics, the abiding feature of all worldly imitations is that they lack dura-bility. In the end the only imitation that will stand is the imitation of our Lord and Savior. One of the greatest threats to this imi-tation is the constant pull away from an eternal perspective to an earthly one.

AN IMITATION WE MUST OUTGROW

In his *Devil's Dictionary*, professional cynic Ambrose Bierce de-fines a Christian as "One who believes that the New Testament is a divinely inspired book admirably suited to the spiritual needs of his neighbor. One who follows the teachings of Christ in so far as they are not inconsistent with a life of sin."[1] As clever as this is, he could've saved some ink and just said "See *hypocrisy*." Of course, hypocrisy is a perennial charge brought against believers from those outside the church, but these days it's also one of the main reasons young people in the church are heading for the exits.[2] While the decline is less precipitous than in years past, the reasons for the departure have grown steadily more serious. Along with the perception of hypocrisy, a growing sense of political alienation is causing numerous young men and women to reconsider the faith of their parents. In this sense the 2016 election is a watershed moment. While it's always tempting to see the challenges of our day as utterly unique, the temptation to become overinvested in our temporal world order is a perennial struggle of humanity through the ages—a frantic search for an imitation that lasts.

F. Scott Fitzgerald's *The Great Gatsby* offers a poignant depiction of this deep longing, with a distinctly American inflection. Gatsby is a kind of self-made man. Born to "shiftless and unsuccessful farm people," James Gatz disowns his legal name, casts off his former identity, and assumes the mantle of Jay Gatsby, a name that "sprang from his Platonic conception of himself."[3] But Gatsby believes he can do more than reinvent himself; he believes he can turn back the clock and reclaim some cherished past. For years he has steadily nurtured an impossible love for Daisy Miller, a flame of his youth who went on to marry a brutal and unfaithful man. Through a friendship with her cousin, Nick Carraway (the novel's narrator), he hopes to pull her back into his orbit. Slowly, we learn that he has arranged his entire life around Daisy. But, as Nick tragically observes, it's no longer Daisy that Gatsby desires but the ideal Daisy. When they finally meet again, we are told that she "tumbled short of his dreams—not through her own fault, but because of the colossal vitality of his illusion."[4] It's a kind of romance we know all too well.

One of the most moving exchanges in the book takes place between Gatsby and Nick as they discuss his plans for Daisy. After warning Gatsby that he needs to temper his expectations because he "can't repeat the past," Gatsby responds, "Can't repeat the past? Why of course you can!" Nick then tells us, "He looked around wildly, as if the past were lurking here in the shadow of his house, just out of reach of his hand."[5]

Gatsby is animated by an Edenic longing that aims to restore the world to some former state of purity and innocence. As idealistic as this may sound, its outworkings are deeply practical. For some, it's as if the desired past were lurking here in the shadow of the White House. For others, Eden lies well down the road and will require an arduous journey. Broadly speaking, two powerful expressions of this Edenic longing manifest as either nostalgia (we need to return to an idyllic past) or utopian fantasy (we need to work together to establish a blissful future world). But the keys to Eden are not to be found anywhere in this world. Eden is not our destination.

The late Roger Lundin reminds us,

> The Bible begins in a garden and ends in a city. . . . That's why we can't go back to the innocence of the childhood we have lost. The way back is barred. The Christian life is about the way forward, but the way forward is the way forward through the cross and the empty tomb. The older I get the less nostalgic I become and the more I become oriented towards the future.[6]

Nick Carraway is right. We can't repeat the past. But Lundin is also right. As Christians, we move forward through the cross and the empty tomb toward a heavenly city that infinitely exceeds all of our quaint, terrestrial aspirations. Jay Gatsby is an illusion, but the life that Christ offers to us—the one he has crafted with the finesse of an artist—is one with a destination and one where growth and maturity don't come at the cost of death. As Paul tells us, the body that is sown perishable is raised imperishable (1 Corinthians 15:42).

If we would learn from Gatsby's example, we must learn to outgrow him.

CHRISTIAN DISCIPLESHIP AND THE CULTIVATION OF HOLY AMBIVALENCE

As a little boy my son, Dylan, watched me with awe as I mowed the grass. The look in his eyes almost made me believe I was the god he thought I was. At the time he had his own mower—a charming little toy that was fueled with soap and produced an iridescent bouquet of bubbles that floated away like stray balloons whenever it was pushed. Together, we pursued our suburban husbandry, my mower shooting out jets of fragrant grass, and Dylan's, evanescent bubbles. I smiled, neighbors laughed, and my wife aimed her phone in our direction; we were just so adorable. But I also remember when she told me that Dylan had repeated one of my carelessly muttered expletives for the benefit of the entire daycare staff. And I remember Dylan observing my fit(s) of road rage from the shelter of his car seat, eyes wide, taking it all in. The look in his eyes almost made me believe I was the devil he saw at that moment.

There's a deeply practical aspect to Paul's exhortation for us to imitate God as "beloved children." For better or for worse, that's precisely what kids do. They imitate the people closest to them. In the case of small children, that's usually Mom and Dad. There's a pronounced temptation to outsource a child's spiritual education to spiritual experts (pastors, counselors, youth workers, conference speakers, etc.) who are supposedly better equipped to handle the complex challenges they face. While we're grateful for the help of those who minister to young people, this help cannot take the place of a parent's responsibility to their child. Even with the best of intentions, this maneuver amounts to an abdication of one's calling. We may not be able to parse the latest statistics from Pew Research, and we may not follow all of the exotic new trends punctuating youth culture, but none of this changes the fact that the Lord has entrusted the stewardship of our children to us. Contrary to popular opinion, a child's spiritual education does not belong to experts; it belongs to their parents. How do we as parents carry out this spiritual education? In a word, through proper imitation—and as we'll see, proper imitation is discipleship.

If we survey the Pauline descriptions of Christ's followers, a kind of poetics of discipleship emerges. In the concluding verses of Romans 13, Paul exhorts his readers to "cast off the works of darkness and put on the armor of light" (v. 12). To this fetching metaphor Paul adds an even more striking phrase: "Put on the Lord Jesus Christ, and make no provision for the flesh, to gratify its desires" (v. 14). Rather than give us a purely negative vision of abstemiousness—a rigid list of don'ts for stifling the flesh—Paul offers these vivid portraits of a Christlike demeanor, comparing our comportment to a kind of sacred garment. Christian disciples, Paul is saying, are those who are wearing Christ. Few things are as practical and visible as the clothes we wear. Why then do so many of us assume that Christlikeness is something private and largely inconspicuous, an inward conviction reserved exclusively for "sacred" spaces like churches and prayer meetings?

But Paul doesn't limit his metaphors to clothing. Indeed, his descriptions of Christian devotion span the gamut of the senses, engaging the heart, mind, and imagination of his readers. To this end he calls Christians a fragrant "aroma of Christ" (2 Corinthians 2:15). Later, Paul calls the Corinthian converts "letter[s] from Christ" (2 Corinthians 3:3) and in his epistle to the Ephesians he calls us Christ's "workmanship, created in Christ Jesus for good works, which God prepared beforehand, that we should walk in them" (2:10). As this rich imagery makes plain, Christians do much more than offer a message or a worldview to a hungry world; we offer a vision: our lives tell the story of the life, death, and resurrection of Jesus Christ. I think of the words of one of the elders at my church as he served me Communion: "Taste and see that the LORD is good, brother" (Psalm 34:8).

Dallas Willard offers a shrewd observation about discipleship: "Another important way of putting this is to say that I am learning from Jesus to live my life *as he would live my life if he were I*. I am not necessarily learning to do everything he did, *but I am learning how to do everything I do in the manner that he did all that he did*."[7] Willard is making a crucial distinction. To see its practical outworking, let's apply it to my misguided middle school efforts. In essence the problem with my Rich imitation was simple: I wasn't Rich. Lacking his knowledge, background, and skills, my bald mimicry was doomed to failure. If, on the other hand, I had learned how to do everything *I* did in the *manner* that Rich did what he did, I would've succeeded—much to my detriment.

A disciple, however, has learned Willard's distinction and knows that a manner of life can be embodied only if it's properly integrated into one's own personality. Let's call to mind Paul's startling image of "putting on Christ" once more. Clothing offers a uniquely intimate picture of a person's peculiar manner because everybody wears it differently. An entire student body may wear the same school uniform, but it will look different on each person. Common clothing cannot efface individuality, and this fact is registered by the diverse shapes and contours of our very bodies. Similarly, if I want to imitate Christ by "learning to live my life as he would live my life if he were I," I need to think creatively about what it means to put him on, to wear him. Though we're united in our purpose to love God supremely and love our neighbor as ourselves, we will each wear Christ uniquely. Your particular gifts, voice, and personality are not accidents—they are integral to Christ's workmanship in your life.

Since the word *disciple* is in danger of being overspiritualized, let's explore it in practical terms. The relationship between a mentor and protégé is a picture of discipleship. From sommeliers to sculptors, skilled craftspeople are always disciples, and their exquisite degree of refinement points back to a rigorous period of apprenticeship with a teacher. For Christian disciples, Christ is that teacher, and all of the lovely qualities that Paul outlines in his letters point back to our divine tutelage. The implications here have a deeply practical bearing on our day-to-day lives: "A successful baseball player who expects to excel in the game without adequate exercise of his body is no more ridiculous than the Christian who hopes to be able to act in the manner of Christ when put to the test without the appropriate exercise in godly living."[8] Though we each wear Christ differently, the spiritual protocol prescribed by Scripture forms a crucial point of unity. It's impossible to overstate the pedigree of the spiritual curriculum, which we commonly call the spiritual disciplines. In Willard's words, "The disciplines for the spiritual life, rightfully understood, are time-tested activities consciously undertaken by us as new men or women to allow our spirit ever-increasing sway over our embodied selves."[9] Through prayer, fasting, silence, study, contemplation, acts of mercy, and many more, Christ's disciples learn the practical implications of the colossal truth that it is no longer they who live but Christ in them.

Discipleship is a basic feature of human life. All of us are disciples. The only question is the person we choose to follow. All of the teachers Rich chose to follow were skilled athletes, streetwise, and thoroughly committed to the notion that we are the masters of our own destiny. As misguided as this is, it's a default mindset for many of us. Though the deep motivations of his heart were inscrutable to mortal eyes, Rich's discipleship was readily evident to all of us. It's part of what drew me to him in the first place. So what stopped me from making him my teacher?

In chapter four my dad told you his stories about the "bad man" that culminated with that revelation that said bad man was in fact none other than himself. Though I wouldn't have articulated it like this at the time, this was my first encounter with spiritual transformation. I simply couldn't reconcile the hardened criminal I had in my mind with the loving dad who sat on the foot of my bed. Yet I knew my dad to be honest; I trusted him. For the first time I saw a converted person for the miracle that they are. Instinctively, I knew that this kind of transformation cannot happen unless a person is changed at their very core. Nothing changes the core of a person but the living God. I also knew it doesn't happen overnight.

We often place a high premium on radical conversion stories while ignoring the long, unglamorous road of spiritual recovery. Growing up I had the tremendous privilege of seeing my parents grow in Christ. They weren't perfect, but I saw them with their heads in their Bibles; I saw the way they welcomed strangers into our home and fed and clothed them and nursed them back to health if they were sick. I knew that my dad's extensive travels were concentrated on spreading the gospel, strengthening believers, and repairing the divisions in the church. Though both of my parents had been imprisoned for their faith, this steadfast commitment was evident in the seemingly insignificant moments, from wrangling us for church on a Sunday morning to Mom's insistence on the necessity of us sharing family meals at the table. These stray moments were anything but trivial, mundane, and quotidian; they were as sacred and precious as the kind of joy that can't be extinguished by the dolorous precincts of a prison cell.

To Christ alone belongs the only kind of discipleship that is inexhaustible. The riches of his love will never fail us. They can and will transform a prison cell into a palace, a hardened criminal into a loving dad. By wearing Christ, my mom and dad communicated to me in word and deed the only kind of discipleship that has true permanence. They were following Paul's blessed injunction: "Be imitators of me, as I am of Christ" (1 Corinthians 11:1). As captivating as Rich was, his thin charade paled in comparison.

Given Paul's highly practical reading of discipleship, let's consider the qualities that ought to characterize our public life as Christians. How might we repair the daunting generational rift and join together as parents and children in our common life together, even in the face of serious differences?

James K. A. Smith offers a powerful rejoinder to our short-sightedness, calling for Christians to recover "a kind of holy ambivalence about our relationship to the political, a sort of engaged but healthy distance rooted in our specifically eschatological hope, running counter to progressivist hubris, triumphalistic culture wars, and despairing cynicism."[10] With this quote, Smith has deftly outlined four political postures: (1) holy ambivalence, (2) progressivist hubris, (3) triumphalistic culture wars, and (4) despairing cynicism. Before we consider "holy ambivalence," it's worth exploring the remaining three, because they each constitute serious temptations for all of us.

Though we may be tempted to immediately associate it with the various radical approaches to freedom and human identity that run the gamut from sexual revisionism to the numerous transhumanist projects gaining traction among our cultural elites, progressivist hubris fits well with any philosophy that sees humanity as the measure of all things. In this sense it taps into that deeply American pursuit of prioritizing the journey over the destination, essentially arguing that we're always moving forward, never looking back, and, on principle, never arriving at a permanent place. Seen in this light, plenty of so-called Christians embrace a version of this political philosophy. It crops up whenever we see our lives like our own and try to take hold of a version of Christianity that offers minimal interference with our preferences.

Triumphalistic culture warring also cuts across political divides, and it arises from a sense of moral superiority. In *The Coddling of the American Mind*, Jonathan Haidt and Greg Lukianoff identify a corrosive mindset that's informing the growing tribalism on university campuses and the wider culture—namely, the belief that life is a battle between good people and evil people.[11] Here, we don't want to be naive. History repeatedly teaches us that few things are as dangerous as an unassailable conviction of one's moral superiority. Such a mindset can be a recipe for chaos since it removes all constraints on general principle. If we're dealing with people we believe to be misguided or misinformed, we can continue to aim at persuasion. If we're dealing with "evil" people, we can enter into an "ends justify the means" frame of mind. Recall Alan Jacob's use of the vivid phrase from the anthropologist Megan Phelps-Roper: the person(s) occupying the "evil" side of our political divides is our "repugnant cultural other"—a designation that sounds appropriately sci-fi in its utterly alien connotations.[12] Once again, a more revealing question for Christians is whether we can make the leap from "repugnant cultural other" to neighbor.

With the proliferation of headlines highlighting the appalling scale of moral degradation in our leading cultural institutions has come a fashionable emphasis on despairing cynicism. Indeed, the notion of strategic withdrawal from culture has birthed a veritable cottage industry in the world of publishing.[13] Since it tends to focus on the spiritual decay of our culture, this posture is much more prevalent among religious-minded people, those who belong to high church traditions in particular. For all my reservations I'll confess that in my darker moments I find this option compelling, and I remain somewhat sympathetic to it. There's good reason, for instance, for Christians to take into careful consideration what it means to belong to Christ rather than the world, and consider how many of our well-meaning outreach efforts often lead to compromise and assimilation. All too often our efforts at reaching Christianity's "cultured despisers" terminate in our own seduction. Given the current state of the North American church, we can't afford to be naive about our susceptibility to temptation.

However, cynical withdrawal can and often does foster a spiritual elitism that's a close cousin of the "life is a battle between good people and evil people" mindset. In this version we see ourselves as a blessed remnant who must flee the surrounding squalor to preserve our spiritual integrity. While it's true that we are set apart and "in the world but not of it," we must not allow our political posture to descend into a sense of moral superiority. Not one of us is exempt from the human condition, and God help us if we think we are. Times of strategic withdrawal have their legitimacy, but we cannot indulge in a political posture that fails to recognize our cultural and political opponents as neighbors.

Holy ambivalence is a marvelous term for capturing the needed political balance: To those who naively champion a progressive journey without a destination, Christians offer a reminder that what we desire is nothing less than a heavenly city, and that this is our destination (Hebrews 11:16). To those who fly the culture-war banner, Christians offer a stark warning against the dangers of overlooking our heavenly citizenship and confusing earthly kingdoms with the kingdom of God. To those who offer a counsel of despair and withdrawal, whether it's cloaked in hopelessness masquerading as realism or spiritual elitism masquerading as piety, Christians offer a reminder that "church is not a soul-rescue depot that leaves us to muddle through the regrettable earthly burden of 'politics' in the meantime; the church is a body politic that invites us to imagine how politics could be otherwise."[14] No matter the news or current upheavals, Christians can confidently affirm the conviction that Christ's consummation of history will usher in the restoration of all things—and recognize that it is the very height of realism.

In Acts 1 the disciples ask their risen Lord about his political agenda for their nation, "Lord, will you at this time restore the kingdom to Israel?" (v. 6). David Gooding points out that the full scope of this question is contained in the unblushing prophecy of Joel 2:28-32, where we are told of the "terrible day of the Lord, when God would 'restore the fortunes of Judah and Jerusalem,' visit the gentile nations with apocalyptic judgment, break their domination over Israel, and restore Jerusalem as the centre of the divine presence."[15] You might say that Christ responds with blessed ambivalence: "It is not for you to know times or seasons that the Father has fixed by his own authority. But you will receive power when the Holy Spirit has come upon you, and you will be my witnesses in Jerusalem and in all Judea and Samaria, and to the end of the earth" (Acts 1:7-8). But these words aren't the full response:

> And when he had said these things, as they were looking on, he was lifted up, and a cloud took him out of their sight. And while they were gazing into heaven as he went, behold, two men stood by them in white robes, and said, "Men of Galilee, why do you stand looking into heaven? This Jesus, who was taken up from you into heaven, will come in the same way as you saw him go into heaven." (Acts 1:9-11)

Christ's ascension offers a picture of our engagement with the world—a picture of holy ambivalence in action, encompassing both Christ's immanence and transcendence. To those who do nothing but stare expectantly into the heavens, the angels reply, "This Jesus . . . will come in the same way as you saw him go into heaven." Therefore, we don't loiter; we wait. Our mission is to be Christ's witnesses to the very ends of the earth, and we go about this business with the full knowledge that he is returning to "judge the living and the dead" and to "wipe away every tear." Neither justice nor mercy will be forsaken. For this reason our political thinking is never a counsel of despair but one of fierce, stubborn, and realistic hope—hope borne of the conviction that our Lord has not abandoned his throne. But Christ's ascension also protects us from the kind of zealous overcommitment to earthly causes that easily calcifies into idolatry. This is why the myriad failures of our leaders and institutions are sources of grief and lament. However, they ought not to leave us in despair. After all, if our final hope is in Christ and his coming kingdom, that hope remains secure, even in the face of surrounding calamities. Regarding our cultural engagement, political and otherwise, holy ambivalence means we avoid total immersion while remaining invested. This is part of what it means to be in the world but not of it. Given its bodily nature, Christ's ascension affirms the rugged and earthy aspects of our mission.

We can and must get our hands dirty for the kingdom. But Christ has also transcended the earthly realm and has ascended his throne, and this grants us the eternal perspective (apocalyptic realism) on our earthly existence. This eternal perspective in turn grants us an indefatigable ability to both inhabit and transcend our circumstances, no matter how dire, because it is rooted in the reality of Christ's kingship.

CONCLUSION

Building the Culture of Your Home

The one constant of Cameron's childhood was an obscure town in the center of Alabama. His mother's parents settled in the area in the 1970s, and the McAllister family would visit them from Austria roughly every three years. At the time it was all they could afford. If you were a kid, there wasn't much to do there but wander and daydream, which was just fine with Cameron. He wanted as little interference with his imagination as possible in those days, and this little town was practically built for childhood reveries.

When the McAllisters moved to the United States in 1998, their lives felt chaotic. The entire country of Austria is about the population of a large American city, and coming to the States felt like entering into a kind of fantasy realm like Jonathan Swift's Brobdingnag, where everything was bigger, louder, and stronger. All of it, that is, except for this small Alabama town, where nothing seemed to change. Sure, a neighborhood would pop up here and there and the occasional factory would close, but the overall scenery remained largely as it had always been. Old white houses with roomy porches and men with Lion's Club hats on their hoary heads waving at passing cars. The blast of a train horn. Fields baked to a weary yellow by the fever of Alabama heat. The old cemetery with its effusion of artificial flowers.

Then there was the grandparents' house with its profusion of sights, smells, and sounds that remained gloriously unchanged. This was Cameron's childhood Eden.

Cameron recently had to return to this little town. Naturally, he's no longer the young daydreamer he was then. He has two children of his own these days, one of them is so much like him it's as terrifying as it is surreal. For Cameron, watching his son's penetrating gaze rove over this memory-laden territory is a bit like time travel. The train horn panics him just as it used to panic Cameron, and the wealth of strange relics and antiques in the grandparents' old home is just as enticing to his nimble hands.

But, of course, this town is not Eden. The only thing growing here these days is the cemetery. The grandparents' house is now as dilapidated as the shuttered storefronts in the town center. Cameron's grandfather is long gone, and his grandmother's condition grows more precarious by the day. The place no longer feels constant to Cameron—it feels stagnant, ossified, and dying. No longer a picture of Eden, he now sees it as a vision of the transience of this world. As painful as it is, it's a vision he desperately needs because, like most Americans, he needs to grow up. An integral part of that growing up involves the recognition that this world is not our home.

Recall Roger Lundin's wise words, "The Bible begins in a garden and ends in a city. That's why in human life our goal can't be to go back to the innocence and the childhood we have lost. The way back is barred: the Christian life is about the way forward. But the way forward is the way through the cross and the empty tomb." Lundin himself died shortly after he spoke these words. His final statement is as haunting as it is challenging: "The older I get the less nostalgic I become and the more I become oriented towards the future."[1]

In Colossians 1:28, Paul gives voice to his spiritual aspiration to present "everyone mature in Christ." Though the language of outgrowing God and faith is now a full-fledged secular trope, it's predicated on a naive understanding of religion in general and the Christian faith in particular. If Christ is indeed the infinite Lord of all creation in whom all things hold together, it's impossible to outgrow him. Indeed, this is simply a category mistake. Becoming like him is such a colossal undertaking that it required nothing less than Christ's death and resurrection.

From Ralph Waldo Emerson to former First Lady Michelle Obama, Americans love the idea of *becoming*, of pursuing our vision of flourishing with as little interference as possible. But this restless pursuit of individual freedom and becoming puts us on a journey without a destination, one that turns us all into spiritual adolescents who can't see beyond the horizon of this world. Christians affirm the centrality of becoming in human life, of course, but they deny the individualistic spin our culture puts on it. As Lundin makes clear, we are indeed moving forward, but Christ is our destination, our goal, our home. Christians are daily becoming more like their Savior because they know that one day they will see him face-to-face.

The strategies outlined in this book will be largely futile if the homes in which they're practiced already belong to a culture at odds with Christ and his church. It remains incumbent on Christian homemakers to build a culture in their homes that reflects the church rather than the surrounding world with its competing myths, stories, and salvation narratives. Step one in this process is the recognition that a culture of the home is inevitable and that it therefore requires a high degree of intentionality. A home that exhibits the culture of the church will be a home shaped by Christ, his Word and the sacraments, and the praise that is due to him. Such a home will always be in tension with the surrounding culture. This healthy tension is conducive to a proper understanding of the temporal nature of the earthly city. It is part of the basic essence of being in and not of the world.

Such a home will also recognize the impermanence of this world. All of the misconceptions we've outlined are predicated on a secular, this-worldly stance. *Information saves* takes for granted that salvation lies in human thought and ingenuity. With its narrow focus on daily circumstances, *fear protects* elevates self-preservation above love and self-sacrifice. Closely aligned with information saves, *spiritual education belongs to experts* outsources Christ's authority to various human professionals.

As Christians we must meet each of these challenges with love and compassion. To those enslaved by fear and uncertainty, our homes must demonstrate that "perfect love casts out fear" (1 John 4:18). To those who believe that information saves, we proclaim Christ "in whom are hidden all the treasures of wisdom and knowledge" (Colossians 2:3). We must seek to know "the love of Christ that surpasses knowledge" (Ephesians 3:19). And to those wavering in their confidence and tempted to outsource Christ's spiritual authority, we boldly profess in his own words, "All authority in heaven and on earth has been given to me. Go therefore and make disciples of all nations, baptizing them in the name of the Father and of the Son and of the Holy Spirit" (Matthew 28:18-19).

In the end the only places abounding in lasting faith are those that belong to Christ. It's our prayer that your home will be such a place and that all those who dwell with you will come to recognize the hallmarks of *his* ownership, rather than yours.

In our lives, in our homes, in our parenting, we are never alone. We leave you with the words of the apostle Paul to the Thessalonians: "Now may the God of peace himself sanctify you completely, and may your whole spirit and soul and body be kept blameless at the coming of our Lord Jesus Christ. He who calls you is faithful; he will surely do it" (1 Thessalonians 5:23-24).

ACKNOWLEDGMENTS

While it's true that not every book has two or more authors, every book is an act of collaboration, and it's a great joy to thank our many collaborators.

To that end, we'd like to begin by thanking our wives, Mary and Heather, both of whom provided love, support, and crucial insights as we labored away on chapter after chapter. This book would not be possible without their voices. Cameron would like to thank his son, Dylan, for the frequent interruptions to "give Daddy a hug" as he sat scratching his head in front of the computer monitor in a makeshift home office during a time of extended quarantine. Those sweet intrusions put flesh and bones on sections that occasionally threatened to become abstract. The arrival of Cameron's daughter, Olivia, two months before the manuscript deadline added a whole new level of joyful urgency to the writing process.

We would like to thank Krin Baer for stimulating conversations, incisive questions, and for poring over large portions of the manuscript. Cameron's chapters especially would not be what they are without his friendship (and Cameron bears full responsibility for whatever defects remain). We would also like to thank our editor, Ethan McCarthy. It's a rare (and sometimes painful) privilege to have a close friend as an editor, and Ethan proved an invaluable (and gentle) voice in the shaping of this book.

Our heartfelt thanks also to the wonderful team at Inter-Varsity Press, who allowed us to make our debut with this book. Equal parts professional and generous, it was a pleasure to work with them.

NOTES

INTRODUCTION

[1]W. H. Auden, *The Dyer's Hand: And Other Essays* (New York: Vintage International, 1989), 21.

[2]The phrase "the shape of our ultimate concern" is lifted from Charles Taylor, *A Secular Age* (Cambridge, MA: Belknap Press, 2007), 427.

[3]The phrase was used in a private conversation between Cameron and Os in 2014. For a full exploration of Guinness's thoughts on culture, see *Renaissance: The Power of the Gospel However Dark the Times* (Downers Grove, IL: InterVarsity Press, 2014), 13-30, 73-89.

[4]William Shakespeare, Sonnet 13, www.poetryfoundation.org/poems/45087/sonnet-18-shall-i-compare-thee-to-a-summers-day.

[5]James K. A. Smith has helpfully compiled these terms into a glossary in his excellent primer *How (Not) to Be Secular*. For those intimidated by Taylor's tome, we'd recommend beginning with Smith's book *How (Not) to Be Secular: Reading Charles Taylor* (Grand Rapids, MI: Eerdmans, 2014). For the glossary, see 140-43.

[6]René Descartes, *The Passions of the Soul*, trans. Stephen Voss (Indianapolis, IA: Hackett Publishing, 1989).

[7]Taylor, *Secular Age*, 140.

[8]Taylor, *Secular Age*, 38.

[9]For an insightful exploration of this issue, see Sherry Turkle, *Alone Together: Why We Expect More from Technology and Less from Each Other* (New York: Basic Books, 2017).

[10]Nicholas Carr, *The Shallows: What the Internet Is Doing to Our Brains* (New York: W. W. Norton, 2010), 206-7.

[11]William Shakespeare, *Hamlet* 1.5.

[12]Taylor, *Secular Age*, 35.

[13]Taylor, *Secular Age*, 35-43.

[14]Gerard Manley Hopkins, *Poems and Prose of Gerard Manley Hopkins*, ed. W. H. Gardner (London: Penguin Books, 1953), 51.

194 *Notes to Pages 11-30*

[15]Hans Boersma, *Heavenly Participation: The Weaving of a Sacramental Tapestry* (Grand Rapids, MI: Eerdmans, 2011), 21. Interestingly, Boersma also draws on Hopkins to illustrate the point, quoting from "God's Grandeur."

[16]C. S. Lewis, *The Voyage of the Dawn Treader* (London: Fontana Lions, 1980), 159.

[17]It's revealing that so many of our illustrations turn on technology. Our constellation of modern conveniences has completely changed the way we view personhood.

[18]Roger Lundin, *Beginning with the Word: Modern Literature and the Question of Belief* (Grand Rapids, MI: Baker Academic, 2014), 112.

[19]Luigi Pirandello, *Six Characters in Search of an Author*, quoted in Lundin, *Beginning with the Word*, 98.

[20]Ralph Waldo Emerson, quoted in Lundin, *Beginning with the Word*, 105.

[21]Michelle Obama, *Becoming* (New York: Crown, 2018), 419.

[22]Andrew Delbanco, *The Real American Dream: A Meditation on Hope* (Cambridge, MA: Harvard University Press, 1999), 97-98.

[23]Walt Disney, quoted in Molly McCormack, "The Big Problem with Disney's Tomorrowland," *AllEars.net*, March 20, 2019, http://allears.net/2019/03/20/the-big-problem-with-disneys-tomorrowland.

[24]Lest you think this a straw man, one of our celebrities recently tweeted: "I love God. I believe in God. But I don't believe my personal beliefs of which we can't confirm should override scientific facts and what we can confirm."

[25]Stanley Hauerwas, *Ware and the American Difference: Theological Reflections on Violence and National Identity* (Grand Rapids, MI: Baker Academic, 2011), 18.

[26]Patrick J. Deneen, *Why Liberalism Failed* (New Haven, CT: Yale University Press, 2018), 48-49.

[27]Joan Didion, *We Tell Ourselves Stories in Order to Live: Collected Nonfiction*, Everyman's Library (New York: Alfred A. Knopf, 2006), 179.

[28]For a haunting meditation on the link between poetry and survival, see Emily St. John Mandel's novel *Station Eleven* (New York: Vintage, 2014).

[29]Albert Camus, *The Myth of Sisyphus*, trans. Justin O'Brien (New York: Vintage Books, 1991), 123.

[30]Delbanco, *Real American Dream*, 114.

[31]Lundin, *Beginning with the Word*, 223.

1. FEAR PROTECTS

[1]Marilynne Robinson, *The Givenness of Things: Essays* (New York: Farrar, Straus and Giroux, 2015), 125.

[2]Alan Jacobs, *How to Think: A Survival Guide for a World at Odds* (New York: Currency, 2017), 26-27.

[3]Greg Lukianoff and Jonathan Haidt, *The Coddling of the American Mind: How Bad Ideas and Good Intentions Are Setting Up a Generation for Failure* (New York: Penguin Press, 2018), 53-77.

[4]Chaucer, quoted in Roger Shattuck, *Forbidden Knowledge: From Prometheus to Pornography* (Orlando: Harcourt Brace, 1996), 166. Shattuck calls this tendency "the Wife of Bath Effect."

2. INFORMATION SAVES

[1]Michael Polanyi, *The Tacit Dimension* (Chicago: University of Chicago Press, 2009), 4.

[2]David Foster Wallace, *Consider the Lobster: And Other Essays* (New York: Back Bay Books, 2006), 144. Given Wallace's considerable gifts as a writer, some readers may see his remarks here as slightly disingenuous. He may not have Austin's skills on the tennis court, but, unlike him, most of us will never know what it feels like to be the recipient of a MacArthur "Genius" Grant.

[3]Wallace, *Consider the Lobster*, 152.

[4]Patrick Radden Keefe, "Anthony Bourdain's Moveable Feast," *New Yorker*, February 13, 2017, www.newyorker.com/magazine/2017/02/13/anthony-bourdains -moveable-feast.

[5]Michael Polanyi, *Personal Knowledge: Towards a Post-Critical Philosophy* (Chicago: University of Chicago Press, 1975), 53; emphasis added.

[6]James K. A. Smith, *Desiring the Kingdom: Worship, Worldview, and Cultural Formation* (Grand Rapids, MI: Baker Academic, 2009), 26.

[7]Blaise Pascal, *Pensées*, trans. A. J. Krailsheimer (New York: Penguin, 1966), 154.

[8]Peter Kreeft, *Christianity for Modern Pagans: Pascal's Pensées Edited, Outlined and Explained* (San Francisco: Ignatius Press, 1993), 232. For a vivid illustration of the distinction between *savoir* and *connaître* drawn from Shakespeare's *Much Ado About Nothing*, see Alan Jacobs, *A Theology of Reading: The Hermeneutics of Love* (Boulder, CO: Westview Press, 2001), 2-8.

[9]Smith, *Desiring the Kingdom*, 32-33.

3. SPIRITUAL EDUCATION BELONGS TO EXPERTS

[1]Harold L. Senkbeil, *The Care of Souls: Cultivating A Pastor's Heart* (Bellingham, WA: Lexham Press, 2019), xvii.

[2]Senkbeil, *Care of Souls*, 115.

[3]Hans Boersma, *Heavenly Participation: The Weaving of a Sacramental Tapestry* (Grand Rapids, MI: Eerdmans, 2011), 21.

[4]Gregory of Nyssa, quoted in Boersma, *Heavenly Participation*, 27.

[5]Peter Kreeft, *Making Sense Out of Suffering* (Cincinnati, OH: Servant Books, 1986), 51.

[6]For an illuminating and hilarious takedown of the self-help cottage industry, see Walker Percy, *Lost in the Cosmos: The Last Self-Help Book* (New York: Picador, 2000).

[7]Augustine, *The Confessions*, trans. Maria Boulding, ed. John E. Rotelle (Hyde Park, NY: New City Press, 2012), 236.

BIOGRAPHICAL INTERLUDE: STUART'S STORY

[1]Alasdair MacIntyre, *After Virtue: A Study in Moral Theory* (Notre Dame, IN: University of Notre Dame Press, 2007), 216.

[2]MacIntyre, *After Virtue*, 216.

[3]*Batman*, directed by Tim Burton (Los Angeles: Warner Bros., 1989).

[4]Blaise Pascal, quoted in Peter Kreeft, *Christianity for Modern Pagans: Pascal's Pensées, Edited, Outlined and Explained* (San Francisco: Ignatius Press, 1993), 28; emphasis added.

4. CULTIVATING DISCERNMENT

[1]Stanley Hauerwas, *With the Grain of the Universe: The Church's Witness and Natural Theology* (Grand Rapids, MI: Baker Academic, 2013).

[2]Czeslaw Milosz, *The Captive Mind*, trans. Jane Zielonko (New York: Vintage International, 1990), 54.

[3]M. Scott Peck, *People of the Lie: The Hope for Healing Human Evil* (New York: Touchstone, 1998).

[4]John Milton, quoted in Karen Swallow Prior, *On Reading Well: Finding the Good Life Through Great Books* (Grand Rapids, MI: Brazos, 2018), 15.

[5]Milton, quoted in Prior, *On Reading Well*, 14-15.

[6]Os Guinness, *God in the Dark: The Assurance of Faith Beyond a Shadow of Doubt* (Wheaton, IL: Crossway, 1996), 23.

5. CULTIVATING LOVE

[1]Dallas Willard, *Knowing Christ Today: Why We Can Trust Spiritual Knowledge* (New York: HarperOne, 2009), 3.

[2]C. S. Lewis, *The World's Last Night: And Other Essays* (Boston: Mariner Books, 2012), 26.

[3]Dallas Willard, *The Renovation of the Heart: Putting on the Character of Christ* (Colorado Springs: NavPress, 2012), 30.

[4]John Stott, *The Radical Disciple: Some Neglected Aspects of Our Calling* (Downers Grove, IL: InterVarsity Press, 2014), 19.

[5]C. S. Lewis, *The Screwtape Letters* (New York: HarperOne, 2001), 28.

⁶James K. A. Smith, *Imagining the Kingdom: How Worship Works* (Grand Rapids, MI: Baker Academic, 2013), 14-15.

6. PUTTING ON CHRIST

¹Hans Boersma, "Fear of the Word," *First Things*, August 2019, www.firstthings .com/article/2019/08/fear-of-the-word.

²Os Guinness, *The Call: Finding and Fulfilling God's Purpose For Your Life* (Nashville: W Publishing, 2018), 5.

BIOGRAPHICAL INTERLUDE: CAMERON'S STORY

¹For a fulsome exposition of the term *expressive individualism*, see Robert N. Bellah, Richard Madsen, William M. Sullivan, Ann Swindler, and Steven M. Tipton, *The Habits of the Heart: Individualism and Commitment in American Life* (Berkeley: University of California Press, 2008), 32-35, 333-34.

²Carcass, "This Is Your Life," *Heartwork*, Earache Records, 1993.

³For a journalistic account of the real-life mayhem behind the scenes, see Michael Moynihan and Didrik Søderlind, *The Lords of Chaos: The Bloody Rise of the Satanic Metal Underground New Edition* (Los Angeles: Feral House, 2003).

⁴See Charles Taylor, *A Secular Age* (Cambridge, MA: Belknap Press, 2007), 322-76. For those intimidated by Taylor's tome, I highly recommend James K. A. Smith's primer *How (Not) to Be Secular: Reading Charles Taylor* (Grand Rapids, MI: Eerdmans, 2014).

⁵Adapted from Cameron McAllister, "Seeing is Bewildering: On the Condition of Cultural Oblivion," RZIM, www.rzim.org/read/rzim-global/seeing-is-bewildering -on-the-condition-of-cultural-oblivion. Used by permission of RZIM.

⁶McAllister, "Seeing is Bewildering."

⁷Philip Larkin, "Church Going," *The Top 500 Poems*, ed. William Harmon (New York: Columbia University Press, 1992), 1,069.

⁸See Philip Salim Francis, *When Art Disrupts Religion: Aesthetic Experience and the Evangelical Mind* (Oxford, UK: Oxford University Press, 2017). It is my contention that this abiding influence shows that the United States is not post-Christian.

⁹Fair warning to adventurous Googlers: this band's visuals are as obscene as they are blasphemous.

¹⁰Charles Taylor, *A Secular Age* (Cambridge, MA: Belknap Press, 2007), 171-76.

¹¹James K. A. Smith, *Desiring the Kingdom: Worship, Worldview, and Cultural Formation* (Grand Rapids, MI: Baker Academic, 2009), 12.

¹²Charles Taylor, quoted in Smith, *Desiring the Kingdom*, 173.

¹³For a crash course, visit Dave Stopera, "What You Think You Look Like Vs. What You Actually Look Like," *BuzzFeed*, May 31, 2012, www.buzzfeed.com/daves4 /what-you-think-you-look-like-vs-what-you-actually.

[14]Blaise Pascal, *Pensées*, trans. A. J. Krailsheimer (New York: Penguin Books, 1967), 67.

7. FAILING SUCCESSFULLY

[1]Mark O'Connell, "Death Watch," *New Yorker*, December 3, 2013, www.newyorker .com/culture/rabbit-holes/deathwatch.

[2]Craig M. Gay, *The Way of the (Modern) World* (Grand Rapids, MI: Eerdmans, 1998), 2.

[3]Spike Jonze's *Her* is a particularly striking example.

[4]Wendell Berry, *Sex, Economy, Freedom & Community* (New York: Pantheon, 1993), 134.

[5]"Practical atheism" is Craig M. Gay's phrase. For an incisive exploration of the topic, see his *The Way of the (Modern) World*.

[6]Berry, *Sex, Economy, Freedom & Community*, 134-35.

[7]In a delightfully snarky comment, Mary Midgley points out that Skinner can be counted among that esteemed group of shy, socially awkward men who attempted to enshrine their temperament as scientific law: "[Skinner's Utopia] is not a scientific dream. It is merely the dream of a shy, unsocial scientist." Mary Midgley, *Evolution as a Religion: Strange Hopes and Strange Fears* (London: Routledge, 2002), 41.

[8]Ralph Waldo Emerson, quoted in Roger Lundin, *Beginning with the Word: Modern Literature and the Question of Belief* (Grand Rapids, MI: Baker Academic, 2014), 105.

[9]John Gray, *Straw Dogs* (New York: Farrar, Straus and Giroux, 2007), 126-27.

[10]Kara Powell and Steven Argue, *Growing With: Every Parent's Guide to Helping Teenagers Thrive in Their Faith, Family, and Future* (Grand Rapids, MI: Baker, 2019), 28.

[11]Hans Boersma, *Heavenly Participation: The Weaving of a Sacramental Tapestry* (Grand Rapids, MI: Eerdmans, 2011), 29.

[12]Leticia Miranda, "An Ivy League Professor Shared a CV of Failures Because You're Not the Only One Who Screws Up," *BuzzFeed*, April 29, 2016, www .buzzfeednews.com/article/leticiamiranda/acad-epic-fail.

[13]*American Beauty*, directed by Sam Mendes (Glendale, CA: Dreamworks, 1999).

[14]"Discernment," *Online Etymology Dictionary*, accessed May 5, 2019, www.etymonline .com/search?q=discernment.

[15]See the Gemological Institute's website: https://4cs.gia.edu/en-us/4cs-diamond -quality.

[16]"Diamond Cut," Gemological Institute of America, accessed June 2, 2020, https://4cs.gia.edu/en-us/diamond-cut.

[17]James K. A. Smith, *Desiring the Kingdom: Worship, Worldview, and Cultural Formation* (Grand Rapids, MI: Baker Academic, 2009), 92.

[18]Richard Bauckham, quoted in Smith, *Desiring the Kingdom*, 92.

[19]For the full transcript, see David Foster Wallace, "This Is Water," *FS* (blog), 2005, https://fs.blog/2012/04/david-foster-wallace-this-is-water.

[20]See Rod Dreher, *The Benedict Option: A Strategy for Christians in a Post-Christian Nation* (New York: Sentinel, 2017).

[21]Walker Percy, *Signposts in a Strange Land* (New York: Picador, 2000), 164.

[22]Dallas Willard, *The Spirit of the Disciplines: Understanding How God Changes Lives* (New York: HarperOne, 1991), 74.

[23]Willard, *Spirit of the Disciplines*, 70.

[24]Willard, *Spirit of the Disciplines*, 32.

[25]Willard, *Spirit of the Disciplines*, 71.

[26]Willard, *Spirit of the Disciplines*, 72.

8. LOVING VIRTUOUSLY

[1]The notion that the cross mitigates divine violence only serves to underscore the deep biblical ignorance of our time. Since the cross is the ultimate site of divine violence, repairing to its bloody precincts whenever we're confronted by God's wrath amounts to little more than begging the question.

[2]Opening epigraph to Walker Percy's *The Moviegoer* (New York, Vintage International, 1998).

[3]Percy, *Moviegoer*, 11.

[4]Percy, *Moviegoer*, 13.

[5]Percy, *Moviegoer*, 10.

[6]Dallas Willard, *The Divine Conspiracy: Rediscovering Our Hidden Life in God* (New York: HarperOne, 1997), 416.

[7]Willard, *Divine Conspiracy*, 415-16.

[8]David Foster Wallace, *Conversations with David Foster Wallace*, ed. Stephen J. Burn (Jackson: University Press of Mississippi, 2011), 59.

[9]David Foster Wallace, *Infinite Jest* (New York: Little, Brown, 2006), 107.

[10]For an exploration of Wallace's Augustinian overtones, see James K. A. Smith, *Imagining the Kingdom: How Worship Works* (Grand Rapids, MI: Baker Academic, 2013), 22-27.

[11]Wallace, quoted in *Conversations with David Foster Wallace*, 24.

[12]"He is also a person who has ordered his love, so that he does not love what it is wrong to love, or fail to love what should be loved, or love too much what should be loved less (or love too little what should be loved more), or love two things

equally if one of them should be loved either less or more than the other, or love things either more or less if they should be loved equally." Augustine, *St. Augustine on Christian Teaching*, trans. R. P. H. Green (Oxford: Oxford University Press, 2008), 21.

[13]Wallace, *Infinite Jest*, 107.

[14]William Dyrness, *Poetic Theology: God and the Poetics of Everyday Life* (Grand Rapids, MI: Eerdmans, 2011), 155.

[15]David Foster Wallace, quoted in Zadie Smith, *Changing My Mind: Occasional Essays* (New York: Penguin, 2009), 286.

[16]Wallace, *Infinite Jest*, 347.

[17]Wallace, *Infinite Jest*, 369.

[18]Leslie Jamison, *The Recovering: Intoxication and Its Aftermath* (New York: Little, Brown, 2018), 7.

[19]Wallace, *Infinite Jest*, 349.

[20]Thomas Hopko, "55 Maxims of the Christian Life," Holy Cross Orthodox Church, accessed June 3, 2020, https://holycrossoca.org/newslet/0907.html.

[21]Wallace, *Infinite Jest*, 350.

[22]Wallace, *Infinite Jest*, 349.

[23]C. S. Lewis, *The Weight of Glory* (New York: HarperCollins, 2001), 26.

[24]Smith, *Imagining the Kingdom*, 2.

[25]John Bunyan, *The Pilgrim's Progress* (Old Tappan, NJ: Spire Books, 1971), 46.

[26]Bunyan, *Pilgrim's Progress*, 52.

[27]Bunyan, *Pilgrim's Progress*, 53.

[28]John Bunyan, quoted in William Dyrness, *Poetic Theology: God and the Poetics of Everyday Life* (Grand Rapids, MI: Eerdmans, 2011), 161.

[29]Adapted from Cameron McAllister, "Worthy to See," previously printed in *Just Thinking: The Quarterly Magazine of RZIM* 21.3, www.rzim.org/read/just-thinking -magazine/worthy-to-see. Used by permission of RZIM.

[30]Dante Alighieri, *The Divine Comedy: The Inferno, The Purgatorio, and The Paradiso*, trans. John Ciardi (New York: New American Library, 2003). *Paradiso* XXXIII, 33, 99, my emphasis.

[31]Alighieri, *Paradiso* XXXIII, 116.

[32]Lewis, *The Weight of Glory*, 39.

[33]Lewis, *The Weight of Glory*, 29-30, 40-41.

[34]Alighieri, *Paradiso* XXXIII, 109-114, my emphasis.

[35]C.S. Lewis, *Prince Caspian* (Glasgow, United Kingdom: William Collins Sons & Co. Ltd., 1951), 124.

9. IMITATING RIGHTEOUSLY

[1]Ambrose Bierce, *The Devil's Dictionary* (Oxford: Oxford University Press, 1999), 25.

[2]Griffin Paul Jackson, "The Top Reasons Young People Drop Out of Church," *Christianity Today*, January 15, 2019, www.christianitytoday.com/news/2019/january/church-drop-out-college-young-adults-hiatus-lifeway-survey.html.

[3]F. Scott Fitzgerald, *The Great Gatsby* (New York: Scribner, 2004), 98.

[4]Fitzgerald, *Great Gatsby*, 95.

[5]Fitzgerald, *Great Gatsby*, 110.

[6]Roger Lundin, "Modern Literature," *YouTube*, December 16, 2014, www.youtube.com/watch?v=kdmQw8FlG_o.

[7]Dallas Willard, *The Divine Conspiracy: Rediscovering Our Hidden Life in God* (New York: HarperOne, 1998), 283; emphasis added.

[8]Dallas Willard, *The Spirit of the Disciplines: Understanding How God Changes Lives* (New York: HarperOne, 1991), 5.

[9]Willard, *Spirit of the Disciplines*, 86.

[10]James K. A. Smith, *Awaiting the King: Reforming Public Theology* (Grand Rapids, MI: Baker Academic, 2017), 16.

[11]Jonathan Haidt and Greg Lukianoff, *The Coddling of the American Mind: How Good Intentions and Bad Ideas Are Setting Up a Generation for Failure* (New York: Penguin Press, 2018), 53-77.

[12]Alan Jacobs, *How to Think: A Survivor's Guide for a World at Odds* (New York: Currency, 2017), 82-83.

[13]Some of the titles here include Rod Dreher, *The Benedict Option: A Strategy for Christians in a Post-Christian Nation* (New York: Sentinel, 2017); Anthony Esolen, *Out of the Ashes: Rebuilding American Culture* (Washington, DC: Regnery, 2017); and Charles J. Chaput, *Strangers in a Strange Land: Living the Catholic Faith in a Post-Christian World* (New York: Henry Holt, 2017).

[14]Smith, *Awaiting the King*.

[15]David Gooding, *True to the Faith: The Acts of the Apostles: Defining and Defending the Faith* (Coleraine, Northern Ireland: Myrtlefield House, 2013), 42.

CONCLUSION

[1]Roger Lundin, "Modern Literature," *YouTube*, December 16, 2014, www.youtube.com/watch?v=kdmQw8FlG_o.